Food is Love

Life, Humor and Sustenance for the Southern Soul

Margie M. Rigney

Published; 2011

No part of this book may be copied or reproduced without permission from the author, except by a reviewer who may quote brief excerpts in a review.

Cover design, photography and graphics by Margie M. Rigney

Formatting, editing and book layout by David L. Rigney jr.

<u>Special thanks to the following wonderful cooks for their recipes</u>:

Nancy G. Miller

Elizabeth (Libby) Alexander

Inza Louise Biggerstaff

Carolyn Rigney

Grace C. Miller

Sweet Tea Publishing

Georgetown, Kentucky

~Dedication~

This book is dedicated to all the men and women out there that manage to keep good food on the table, a hug in their arms and a smile on their face, even in times of adversity.

To those fellow hunters and gatherers that juggle jobs, grocery lists, children, school carnivals, homework, the family dog, dental appointments, soccer and basketball games yet still manage to get the lawn mowed every Saturday morning and the garbage out on Sunday night... You are my hero. You keep the world turning and make perfect sense of it all.

To my husband David, my beautiful children; William, Ben and Lydia, my sister Lisa, wonderful parents, in-laws, family and friends that believed in me, thank you for your appetites, love and humor.

In butter we trust.

~Margie

"Bacon is the Jell-O of the meat world"

~Margie Rigney

Table of Contents:

Introduction: 10

Food is Love: 11

Let's Start off with Good Friends: 12

(Nancy's coffee break cake) 15

From Ha-ha's to Ta-ta's: 16

(Southern Hashbrown Casserole) 19

Shaken but not Disturbed: 20

(Margie's Beer Cheese) 22

The Whole Truth and Nothing but: 23

(Rigney kids favorite Meatloaf) 28

President of the Aspergum Club: 29

(Cinnamon Kugel) 33

Finding Starbucks... a coffee addicts
pursuit of the Holy Grail: 34
(Drunk Raisin Bread;Southern Scones) 38

The Loud Lullaby...testimony of a
snorer's wife: 39
(Too Tired Tater Tot Casserole) 41

Mamas Lessons: 42
(Watergate Salad) 46

Lunch Lady Love: 47
(Real chicken with bones!) 51

The Bible School Junkie: 52

(Mushroom Baptized Chicken Pot Pie).......................55

"How I killed my first hot dog":................................56
(Microwave Applesauce Bars).................................61

Thank God for Baby Wipes:......................................62
(Chocolate Chip Pie)

Me and the Big ol' Boy-an iron skillet love affair.......67
(Iron Skillet Pineapple Upside Down Cake)...............69

Groundhogs, Pocket-books and
Easter Breakfasts:..71
(Easter Garlic Cheese Grits)...................................74

Zen and the Art of Gardening:................................75
(Oreo Dirt Sundaes)...78

Now Serving-Service with a Smirk:.........................79
(Parmesan Crusted Salmon).....................................83

Camping with the Princess:.....................................84
(One Skillet Camp Supper)..87

A Fumbling, Tumbling, Food
Addicts confession:..88
(I "arta choke you" dip)..90

The Winter of our Contentment:..............................91
(Pizza in a Cup)...94

Green Apple Shampoo and a Spiritual Cleansing:........95
(Sleep over Camp Sloppy Joes)..................................98

Chicken Soup for the Neighborhood:............................99
(Easy one pot chicken noodle soup)..........................102

From Pizza Man to Rocket Science:..........................103
(When life gives you lemons, Lemonade Pie)..............105

Did I Miss my own Mid-Life Crisis?:..........................106
(Peter Peter Pumpkin bread)......................................109

"I be Betty":..110
(Fuhgettaboutit-Slow Cooker Lasagna)....................112

When I get to Heaven, can I ask God for Ice cream?:113
(Heavenly Ice Cream Salad).......................................115

Memories in Brown Corduroy:.................................116
(Dads favorite Cooked Cabbage)..............................117

Halloween, Sugar Comas and Peeping Moms:..........121
(Beans 'n Sweet Cornbread).......................................123

My Mom Jeans Revolution Soundtrack....................126
("Sock it to me" Cake)..130

The Terrible Fours, Fives and Forties.......................131
(Carolyn Rigney's Greek Pot Roast).........................133

De-evolution of Resolutions:....................................134
(Aunt Louise's (Inza's) 7-layer Salad).......................137

King of the Lawn Boys:..138
(Dump cake)...141

Son-Shine on my Shoulders:.....................................142
(Favorite Broccoli Casserole).....................................145

Sweet Scents and Toddling Toes:..............................147
(Kentucky Burgoo)..150

"Because I said so":..152
('Nilla Front Porch Tea)..155

Best Friends and Breadsticks:...................................156
(Aunt Libby's Squash Casserole)..............................159

Fishing for Words:..161

(Kentucky Hot Brown Casserole).....................164

Sweatin' with the Oldie:..................................166
(3 Green Casserole)..169

Thankful, Thankful...Thankfulness:.................170
(Best Ever Cranberry Relish with Red, Red Wine)..174

Stand and Deliver:...175
(Granny Miller's Mayonnaise Drop biscuits)..........178

<u>Biography</u>..180

Let me introduce myself...
****

Well, I would have to describe myself like this, I'm just a simple, Southern, stay at home Mom with too much to talk about to keep it to herself. I believe love, laughter, rich food and strong coffee make the world a better place.

I am a stay at home Mom that rarely stays home. I have three kids, a husband, a dog, a guinea pig, two aquariums of fish, sweet parents, two sisters, loving friends and extended family I love dearly and wish lived closer. I try hard to find humor in everything because life is too short not to enjoy it. I've lived a philosophy of *Go big or go home* my entire adult life and it's brought me lots of great memories, more than my share of hangovers and a closet full of plus-size jeans.

Around these parts; *"When the going gets tough, the tough get hungry"*. I think the best cook books are the old ones. You know the ones I'm talkin' about, hand typed copies in spiral form from elementary school PTO's, your grandmother's church, the County Homemakers Club and even the ones your mother made out of index cards and filed away next to the flour and sugar crocks. I believe kids belong in the kitchen, right next to their parents. Passing stories along with recipes and sharing a part of life that has been forgotten thanks to the microwave and invention of the drive -thru window.

There will be no counting calories here, "low-carb' doesn't exist within the folds of these pages. This is stick to your ribs food, not made for the faint of heart or the culinary snob. Where I'm from we enjoy our food and we use it for medicinal purposes, for body and spirit.

My goal of this book is to vent, entertain and opinionate, with a heavy emphasis on the "opine".

In a perfect world, we would all be gathered around a well worn kitchen table in someone's home, kids off to school and each of us holding a steaming hot "cup o' Joe". Ready to take a much deserved coffee break, crack open one another's brains for a *look-see* and a healthy release of whatever ails us.

I invite you to my coffee break. Pull up a chair; laugh, cry, take a moment to leave your own troubles behind and find a little comfort in food and friendship from my kitchen table to yours.

Welcome to my world and as we say in the South...

"Let's chew the fat together."

...Food is love...
:~:~:~:~:~:~:~:~:~~:~:~:

If you're from anywhere below the Ohio River...you've heard it your entire life, "Food is Love".

It's more than a saying with my family, friends and fellow Southerners, in fact, where I come from...it's a way of life.

We are born into a world where a feast of food announces our arrival. Before baby gets home from the hospital, cheese-rich casseroles are being made in their honor, cakes and hot yeasty breads are making their way to the door to welcome the newest family member into the fold.

The same goes when you leave this wonderful world. Food is made to comfort your loved ones and many a shared story of your life here on Earth will be celebrated over an iron skillet of cornbread and a steaming bowl of soup beans.

This is how we do it.

We open up our hearts as well as our appetites and drink it all in. In our part of the world, the good, the bad and the ugly has a side dish and a reason for its existence.

For any occasion, for every need, there is a food that can make it feel better and taste sweeter.

Good food does more than feed the stomach... it can satisfy the soul.

Let's start off with good friends

~:~:~:~:~:~:~:~:~:~:~

As a child born in the 1960's, I grew up sipping the last bitter drops of my mothers "straight" black coffee at a table with her lady friends. This was a daily ritual in our suburban neighborhood. Coffee breaks began as soon as sons and daughters were packed off to school and before most of the women had even had a chance to get the foam rollers and bobby pins out of their hair.

They would gather around well worn, brightly colored, Formica tables, with their ashtrays and saccharin tablets. Donned in scarf wrapped hair to discuss life, recipes, husbands and drink that heavenly aromatic beverage...coffee fresh from the percolator. Automatic drip wasn't even around yet...you wanted good coffee it took a percolator on the counter gurgling and burping for half an hour. But it was worth it, or at least it was worth it to them.

As soon as I was able to stand up straight on my own, I balanced silently behind my mother on the rungs of a kitchen chair while the five of them gossiped, laughed and cried with one another. I was one of the Coffee-Club-Girls, while I was still a toddler and it all seemed completely normal to me.

I would feast on saltines straight from the tin and run my fingers through my Mama's hair while she sipped her coffee. Her friend Betty had nicknamed me "Zesta" because I ate so many crackers. I can remember Mama would let me drink the last drop of cooled coffee from her cup. Bitter and cold, no sugar and terribly strong, but everyday I would take that last sip. I waited patiently for that black gold, that liquid indoctrination into the *coffee club*; it was by all accounts, my daily caffeinated baptism.

My neighbors would ask my mother, "*Nancy, how can you stand that?*" referring to me standing behind her running my fingers along her hairline and dotting her neck with crumbs. She would politely reply, "*Stand what?*" not thinking anything about the forty pound monkey on her back and treating me like I was worthy.

These daily confabs around neighborhood kitchen tables saw them through loving marriages, pregnancies and sons being sent off to Vietnam and Germany, leaving young newlywed wives and babies behind. These wonderful Kentucky women passed through each others lives as beacons and buoys when the storms of life became overwhelming and offered a laugh and a light along the way.

Many of these women shared a need for *mothers little helpers* because it was a period when the world seemed to be crumbling and making no sense. People didn't talk of depression or anxieties, instead they talked of "nerve pills" and the like.

This whole charade was okay to them as they felt a little too upright and Baptist to give in to uncorking a bottle of wine or sipping a little Kentucky bourbon...but they were smart enough to know that they needed a little *something* to get them through this tumultuous time. Sons were ripped from the sides of their families for the draft to fight a war that we couldn't define and it was shown every night at 6 o'clock on the Evening News right after our Jell-O 123 dessert.

Two of these wonderful women would later die of cancer, one would become a widow, one would develop Alzheimer's and my own mother would be overcome with Rheumatoid Arthritis before her fifty-fifth birthday, but all of them celebrated their time together. Their love, admiration and acceptance of one another made me search for that connection most of my adult life and I rejoiced when I found it in the women I now call my friends.

These coffee-fueled ladies of my youth smoked cigarettes to keep their weight down and would skip meals to keep their hour glass figures. They even smoked when pregnant because their docs assured them it was okay. They kept a clean house, wore *polyester everything* and even managed to hang their sheets on the line to dry and had a made-from-scratch dinner ready by 5:00 pm every night.

They did all this and made sense of it. They did this and it makes no sense to me...as I prefer the cork, the shot glass, cotton and the convenience of an electric dryer. I prefer chocolate to cigarettes and I expect to eat when I'm hungry.

I gave up trying to figure out if I'm an "apple shape or a pear"...

...so I just decided to be the basket.

Nancy's "Coffee Break" Cake

This coffee cake makes my heart smile and my house smell like home. Make it the night before or cook it up in minutes before friends come over for coffee or even as a dessert on a warm evening topped with vanilla ice cream.

Ingredients:

For Cake:
2 cups *baking mix**
2/3 cup 2% or Whole milk
2 round TBS of white sugar
1 large egg

1. Heat oven to 375*
2. grease 9" square or round pan generously
3. blend all 4 ingredients with mixer or handmix and spread in pan.

Cake Topping:
1/3 cup baking mix
1/3 cup PACKED brown sugar (light or dark)
1/2 tsp ground cinnamon
2 ½ TBS firm butter (there is no substitute)

1. Mix *baking mix*, brown sugar and cinnamon. Cut in margarine using a fork until mixture is crumbly.
2. Sprinkle on cake mixture in pan evenly.
3. bake 20 minutes or until golden brown.
4. Serve warm. Perk some coffee and enjoy.

*Authors note: *Every good Southern cook has these three things on hand…Jiffy* baking mix (Bisquick or store brand baking mix will do), real butter and brown sugar. You're going to need this "bakers holy trinity" for lots of the recipes in this book, so make sure you stock up.*

From Ha-Ha's to Ta-tas
~:~:~:~:~:~:~:~:~:~:~

I love women. I love the company of good women. The deep camaraderie built up between people of the female persuasion over a cup of coffee or an ice cold Diet Coke is phenomenal. We need only a bridge to cross.

Sometimes we are united in stories of motherhood, triumphs, humor and even shared tragedies. Together, as women, we have the remarkable ability to laugh and embrace not only our own faults but one another's.

God certainly got it right when he made woman.

I'm not saying we are better than men by any means, but we need one another to fill a void that spouses and significant others can't. Not because of any other reason than we are women...

...Above the din of clinking plates, rattling silverware and mumbled coffee-filled conversations, seven Mothers and one small infant gathered at a table in the back of Cracker Barrel to eat breakfast. This wasn't the first of these meetings a 'la eggs and it wouldn't be the last. I was privy to this gathering of the minds and couldn't help but wonder as I sat there amongst these fellow women that shared so much in common with me, why we had not done this sooner.

What began as just a few scattered acquaintances has transpired into a fellowship of females that goes all too often forgotten in our society anymore.

Women need women.

We need that confirmation that we are not only wives, mothers and daughters but have the capability and the desire to support one another even when we think we don't need it. Laughter truly is the best medicine. The endorphins set free during one of our breakfasts are phenomenal and afterwards I feel refreshed and invigorated.

I have been so blessed with the women in my life.

With the invention of the internet and email, I have been able to form friendships through the written word before even meeting in person. Now we have a gang of "*Mamas*" that are meeting once a week or so to vent, laugh and swap tales before embarking on our day of have-to's and want-to's.

Everyone needs friends.

Every person, male or female needs that arena to let out steam, share laughter and lend support and do so without judgment. Even if you have a wonderful marriage, relationship or feel fine on your own, people need people. You may have to break a few eggs, so to speak to find that great combination that works, but when you do, it's priceless.

I am so thankful for my family and friends and my hope is that everyone would be so blessed. I'm not even sure why any of them put up with me sometimes, but for some reason they are blind to my faults and wacky ways.

I love that we come in all sizes, shapes and tints. I love that we can be from anywhere and everywhere but still arrive at the same place. We find common ground that cements us to our dining room chair and makes us connect. Seeing eye to eye isn't mandatory, in fact different perspectives are encouraged. I probably learn more by someone believing I am wrong than I have by being right.

I have the pleasure of spending the occasional breakfast in tears. Not tears of sadness but those of joy. United around a dining room table in a friends home or saddled up to tables in a local eatery; we talk of everything we can reach in and pull out of our bushel basket of all things "female". We've discussed childhood vacations, *pleather* car interior, Stuckey's pecan logs, Spam (the real one in a can), lady beards, waxing down-below, recipes, marriage, divorce, liquid Opiates (this was from my own basket), holiday invites and "un"vites, mail order brides, falling down stairs, real vs. artificial Christmas trees and big boobs, just to name a few.

Nothing is off limits around a table of women like this. We create an absolute "open bar" of snippets to choose from, each of us putting our own favorite breakfast dish on the buffet...these dishes not only come in the form of oatmeal, hash browns, bacon and sliced fruit, but also in the form of conversation starters that can only bloom and flower in a roomful of hormones. Even if some of them are produced in the form of an Estrogen patch, myself being the bearer of this wonderful, adhesive, midlife sidekick.

From *ha-ha's to Ta-ta's* we discuss. We laugh, we query and we encourage. We refill our plates and we refill our cups and when it's all over with I have a happiness hangover. My husband has always appreciated how good morning confabs with my L*adies o' the Round Table Breakfast Club* gives me a sense of self.

Sometimes, I must say, for the faint of heart, I may be a bit over the top. I like to step over the fence just a bit and peek around corners that many women wouldn't. I am an open book with some of the pages torn. There are many women that may not like such a riotous first meal of the day and not everyone thinks I am their cup of tea.

Thank goodness for good coffee, Diet Coke and women that do.

Southern Hashbrown Casserole

Any cook worth their weight in salt has to know how to make a good hashbrown casserole. It sticks to the ribs, tastes better the next day and can make any cold morning a bit warmer saddled up next to a plate of fried eggs and biscuits.

Ingredients:
2 lb. bag of frozen shredded potatoes
1 C. diced onions
1 stick butter
1 pt. Sour Cream
8 oz package of sharp cheddar cheese (shredded)
½ cup small cubed Velveeta cheese
1 can Cream of Chicken soup
½ sleeve of saltines (crushed)
Salt and pepper to taste

1. Preheat oven to 350*
2. Grease an oblong glass dish. (9X11)
3. In a large bowl mix thawed hashbrowns, diced onion, sour cream, cream of chicken soup and cheeses.
4. Pour into well-greased glass dish.
5. Top with crushed Saltines.
6. Top Saltines with one stick of thin sliced butter pats

*Bake uncovered for 40 minutes or until hot, bubbly and brown. Serve with breakfast, brunch or dinner. Great for pot lucks.

"Shaken, but not disturbed"
:~:~:~:~:~:~:~:~:~:~:~:~:~:~:

I live to entertain. I love planning parties, guest lists and friends and family game nights. I look forward to turning off the television and looking only to those I love for my entertainment for the evening.

I enjoy making new cocktails with friends and family. There is something romantic about a drink in a glass that's been shaken and not stirred. Something beautiful about a new bottle of wine breathing in the room and the way a good Red pours into a glass and hugs the inside as it settles into place. I think as I age, I have a finer appreciation for "social lubrication".

I wasn't surprised when I took a test to discover that I would have thrived as a woman in the 1950's. I love donning my apron and getting my *June Cleaver* on, minus the heels and pearls.

The dicing, the slicing and the presentation of well cut vegetables into a bona-fide sunburst of color on an antique cut glass relish tray complete with dip, well it does things to me.

Good things.

During my first years of life in the 1960's so much was happening; as a Nation we were watching Man walk on the moon, women were experiencing sexual freedom thanks to a little plastic pill case and bras were being burned on my behalf long before I would be wearing my first B cup from Sears.

Truly a time to celebrate.

Too bad I was in diapers for the first half and a Brownie uniform for the latter. Having sisters that are 9 and 11 years older than I am, I was privy to seeing life through their eyes and their participation in the *Age of Aquarius*.

I feel like even though I have a 50's heart and yearn for a bit of Sinatra on the turntable now and then, I'd be lying if I said I wouldn't be tempted to experience a bit of the famous 60's and 70's "mellow yellow" hype that slipped by me unappreciated if I could...I think we all have a flower child in us yearning to get out.

I confess fully that I love my family and friends. I love being surrounded by laughter and the giddy feeling of too many cocktails on occasion. I love a good joke and the sweet pop of a fermented cork being plucked from the neck of a bottle that could just as likely be from the finest vineyards in Italy or the bluegrass fields of Kentucky. I love good conversation and witty banter.

For many women, they may think I am old fashioned, but I am by my own standards, the opposite. I appreciate life in general. I often don my headphones and clean house to the poetic stylings of Lil' Wayne and Kanye'. I think I know more R&B than my teenagers.

I'm a pretty modern woman, I just know what I like, when I like it and who I like it with, even if I do it in my grandmothers hand me down apron.

Margie's Beer Cheese

Maybe you've never heard of it, maybe you have, but there is nothing like good beer cheese. You can adjust the "heat" in this recipe by adding or reducing the red pepper and Tabasco sauce. Personally, I think a little heat makes everything taste better!

<u>Ingredients</u>:

7-8 oz of Beer (I use Miller's High Life or Killian's)

Extra Sharp Cheddar Cheese (20 Oz.)Shredded

2 cloves pressed fresh garlic

½ white onion (slice before adding to food processor)

¼ tsp red pepper (add more if you like "heat")

¼ tsp Tabasco sauce

1/8 tsp salt (optional)

Place all ingredients in a food processor and pulse/process until pasty. Place mix in covered bowl and chill overnight. Serve on saltines with carrots and celery sticks. This is a must-have Kentucky Derby classic!

The whole truth and nothing but...
:~:~:~:~:~:~:~:~:~:~:

I love being a mother, even though sometimes to the world I may appear like I'm not that thrilled. My oldest son told me once, he didn't want to grow up, because it looked like being a grown up was all *"have to"* and no fun.

Dang, that sweet boy was right and I had to laugh because a big hunk of adulthood is "have to" but that doesn't mean it's not worth it. Nobody takes up parenting so they can point and stomp and fuss. (Although, I am extremely awesome at it.) Boot Camp ain't got nothin' on this forty-something Kentucky gal.

Believe me if you had told me I would have to wake up my kids three times each morning just to get them out of bed, pick up clothes 24/7, force kids into showers, force them out, nag, complain and nearly pistol whip just to get homework done around here...only to see myself "morph" into some cranky old woman I don't recognize in the mirror- I would probably have had my tubes tied for my 16th birthday gift. But that's part of the Mothering job. It just comes with the territory.

I gave up my Cosmo magazine for Taste of Home, cute shoes for supportive Nikes and because I eat my feelings too much of the time I gave up my girlish figure for one that requires elasticized waist *Mom* jeans. But it's all good, kids need something soft to cry into when they're blue and a big soft hug when they're happy.

I used to be a fairly sane person. I could keep my mind clear, carry on conversations on the phone and knew where my purse was. (*most of the time*) Now, after parenting for 18 years, I forget my makeup, leave the milk in the car, and have to send out scouting parties for my house keys. Sometimes I even wave a crisp one dollar bill at the foot of the stairs, just to attract a posse for the key ring search and award the winner his loot when they usually show up still hanging in the front door knob.

I caught myself sitting alone in the house the other day with Nickelodeon on the television and humming the theme song to Dora the Explorer and my kids outgrew that brown haired lass years ago. My once alert and quick mental agility has now downsized into a small zip folder of what's for dinner, who I dropped off at the library, who needs to bathe next and which bathroom is out of toilet paper.

At the end of the day, the rest of the world looks at me worn, tired and at my wits end and wonders why I ever embarked on this parenting expedition.

I start off looking like a half crazed cave woman most mornings, wielding my finger around pointing and *harrumphing* my way through the house. I bet if I saw myself from a surveillance camera I would be shocked at how ridiculous I look when I'm in full Mama-Mode all cocky and hormonally influenced. I see myself as *June Cleaver*, when in actuality I am probably closer to a *Granny Clampett,* with the figure of a 2 liter.

I see those reality shows with the professional Nannies and their "time out cushions" and "Naughty Spots" and many of the disciplines she calls *mistakes*, are in my kiddo commandments. I have to ask myself, if the offspring on those shows just listen to her because of her strikingly crisp and perky British accent.

I highly doubt she would have the same result taming little Johnny and Savannah if she walked in speaking thick "Kentucky Redneck" and told them to "*get yer hind-quarters in that there time out chair b'fore I yank a knot in yer tail*"...

Forget the Brit Nanny, let's get a weather worn County raised Juanita. A mom o' five who lives in furry slippers and pajama pants from the holler on her own television show; trying to convince 4 year old Jimmy John to stop carrying the cat by the tail, pickin' his nose and eating things he finds in the floorboard of the '84 Dodge pickup. Now that's a reality show I can wrap my head around. In fact, I think I've seen Juanita every time I go to Wal-Mart.

One thing is for sure. Parenting is not easy. But it is rewarding. I used to read all those pregnancy magazines, *Expecting* books and thought I had it all under control before our first wee one even arrived. That bundle of joy we brought home was easy squeasy the first 24 hours... And then he woke up.

I never knew a child could cry so loudly for no apparent reason. But when he cried something awoke in my psyche I didn't even know existed and suddenly, without warning, my heart began to live outside my body. I no longer cared about sleep, eating or basic bodily functions. I was no longer just me, I had become a living feeding station and sleep deprival was my new hobby. My heart was now housed in a red faced, little human that needed me more than I ever realized was possible.

Over the years, I have perfected my early parenting skills, realizing that it's okay for babies to cry on occasion, that they don't self destruct or explode if they are not picked up within 3 seconds after letting out a wail. But without a doubt I have learned that sleep is more important than any of us give it credit. It makes you angry if you don't have it. It brings on depression and its absence ages you about 10 years for every post partum bambino you pop out into the world.

My wonderful kids have made me see the world in a new way. I thought I knew it all until I had kids. Having kids has given me a second childhood and a second chance to get it right. I get to experience Santa Claus, the Easter Bunny and the tooth fairy all over again. Through the years, I have learned lots of things about myself as well as my kids and one thing is for certain, it is all definitely worth it.

Shocking but true.... Things I have learned as a parent:

1. Kids think ketchup is a side dish.

2. That "funky" smell in the car is probably you.

3. Never leave a two year old in the same room as a tube of A&D diaper ointment.

4. Never assume everything is okay just because the kids are

quiet.

5. A&D diaper ointment is really hard to get out of hair and carpet.

6. Some children under two will eat and/or choke on Rugrat stickers, flies in the window sill, carpet fuzz and eat the aluminum foil on chocolate Easter Eggs.

7. My local 911 dispatch team has a fantastic response time.

8. Some toddlers will make their own "paint" from their diaper deposits.

9. Never, ever run out of Pine Sol.

10. Every child thinks their parents were born *before* electricity.

11. All school projects supplies will have to be bought the night before the project is due and 30 minutes before bedtime.

12. When children get a stomach virus, they will never throw up until they are in their beds or in your car.

13. When your child says they *"gotta go now"*.....It's already too late.

14. Any curse words you say will be repeated by your two year old at church or in front of your parents.

15. A teenager will shower until all the hot water is gone and still forget to wash their hair.

16. All children need you the most when you are in the bathroom.

17. All kids are locksmiths, bathroom doorknobs open with a toothpick or the end of a water color paintbrush.

18. *"Bad Hair Day"* always falls on Picture Day.

19. When kids wash their hands, soap is rarely involved and they never replace the toilet paper roll.

And one final epiphany...

20. My kids don't think of their glasses as "half full, or half empty" they just think there's "free refills."

So, maybe growing up is fun. I get to learn all this privileged information from my kids and I get to go to bed every night knowing my husband Dave and I are raising some pretty awesome human beings.

Maybe the best is even yet to come on this roller coaster, but I am already enjoying the ride, even if I look terrified at the turns. I am going to try to show my kids that adulthood is more than *have to* that it is *want-to*. And when things get too hairy, I'll turn on the British accent and see if that works, if nothing else, maybe it will lighten the mood.

And the next time you feel like you are at your wits end, ask yourself if you know where your car keys are, and if you do, you are already one step ahead of me.

Rigney Kid's Favorite Meatloaf

Ingredients:
3-4 lbs of Store ground beef or ground chuck
2 cups of Pepperidge Farm stuffing (any flavor, I prefer Herb or cornbread)
4 eggs
½ cup milk
2 Tbs Worcestershire sauce
1/3 cup BBQ sauce
2 tsp hot sauce
½ cup of diced green pepper
½ cup of diced onion
1/2 cup of ketchup
MIX it up and form into a loaf and transfer to glass baking dish.
Bake at 325* degrees, uncovered until nearly done. (about 40 minutes for one loaf) During final 10 minutes top with the following:

SAGE SAUCE: (I usually make extra for the table)
1 ½ cups of ketchup mixed with the following:
1 tsp hot sauce
2 Tbs ground sage
2 tsp ground mustard **or** 1 Tbs. prepared mustard
2/3 cup of packed brown sugar

In our house, meatloaf is a near religious experience. It is mandatory that it be served with mashed potatoes, peas and something sticky and sweet for dessert. Anything else would be sacrilege.

President of the "Aspergum" club

I'm not sure when child-proof caps were invented, but I can tell you it was well after they should have been, and not during my childhood.

Someone in the mid 1960's came up with the grand idea of delivering doses of the pain reliever "aspirin" via Chiclets shaped chewing gum tiles. It came in a foil card, with a plastic front and a blister-pack backing. You could pop their rectangular, cherry-red or delicious orange little bodies through with very little effort. Every mother I knew carried a pack in their purse.

My mother offered them to me in church if I was fussy or fidgety. I loved the taste of this particular medication. More than once, I found myself in my Mamas cedar closet, nestled in around her dress pumps and shoe boxes in the dark. Rummaging through her shiny patent leather church purse for Aspergum while the hems of her dresses tickled the back of my neck and the faint light of her bedroom sliced through the closed closet door.

I would chew the Aspergum until the crack of the cherry flavored coating was gone and the acidic flavor of aspirin would cut across my tongue and stick in my throat. I enjoyed sneaking, hiding and enjoying my abilities at being such an apt pupil in the school of deceit. I would be a bit nervous, but there was a thrill it gave me to find out that I could get away with something and I was only four or five years old.

As a youngster, I loved vitamins. *Poly-Vi-Sol* circus shapes were my drug of choice. Often times, having older sisters proved to be my best way to get my tasty treats. All I would have to say is *"Mama said I need a vitamin"* and ask one of my older sisters to fetch me one. Then return later to get my other sister to unknowingly repeat the same steps. I look back and can only imagine it was by the grace of God that I didn't die from vitamin and aspirin overdoses.

Since child-proof caps were non-existent, the only child-proofing done in my home was putting things "out-of-reach", but that technique rarely works with any child. Since my mother had chores that took her out of the house, like hanging clothes on the line to dry, I knew just how long I had to get my medicinal errands done. I'd wait 'til she had a basket of sheets to hang and using a chair to get up on the countertop, I would peruse the glass bottles of elixirs in the tall cabinet within seconds of her departure into the suburban jungle.

I remember being so small that when I stood on the countertop I was eye-level with the bottles of cough syrup and stomach medicines my mother believed she had safely hidden.

Fletchers Castoria.

Clear bottle. White cap. Tall neck.

I loved that stuff. It smelled like sweet prune juice and tasted like candy, it still makes my mouth water to think of it. I can remember licking my fingers when I was done. Just a swig or two and taste that rich syrupy goodness. If I wasn't careful, I would nearly get caught, lost in my heavenly apothecary and its inventory, tasting all the potions with my fingers. We had a dog that would go with my mother when she went outside, and always beat my mother to the back door on her return. So when "Boogie" would bark at the back door, that was my cue to end my snooping and shove the chair back across the speckled pink linoleum to the kitchen table.

I loved the garage in our back yard. Our house didn't have an attached garage, it was made of concrete block and my Dad had built it after they moved into their house. It was huge. Sometimes I would rifle through the pockets of my fathers old jackets he had hanging on nails and find half strips of Doublemint gum or peppermints. My father always chewed 1/2 sticks of gum. If you asked for gum, you never got a whole stick. He would say, *"Here ya go, a half stick is more than enough"*...maybe it's because he grew up during the depression that made him covet his little paper wrapped confections but even today he offers only a half stick and he is in his 80's.

Our garage was crazy. For some kids, it probably was the instigator of a few nightmares. My dad had deer antlers and deer feet hanging all over the place, bent, dried and tied with rope that he presumably was going to use as a gun rack later, but never did. Petite pointy feet dotted the exposed ceiling beams in groups of 2 or more from hunting expeditions to Colorado and the Eastern Kentucky mountains. Tiny feet that curled into "L" shapes patiently waiting for their turn to hold a rifle over someone's fireplace. Most likely, displayed just below their own stuffed heads or someone they knew.

It's a wonder I'm not scarred for life. I learned to toughen up at a tender young age...it wasn't uncommon for my dad to hold butchering parties in our back yard in front of the garage after one of his deer hunts or fishing trips. More than once he used my snap-set kiddie-pool filled with water and ice to float just-cut roasts and meat trimmings before they got packaged for the freezer. That's not a sight you forget easily. Bits and pieces of chopped animal carcass silhouetted against the backdrop of *happy fish and seashells on vinyl* has a tendency to stick with you for life.

On one of my garage scavenger hunts in the garage, I found a salt pill gun. This was a hand held plastic device that when you held it in your hand and squeezed the trigger a small white pill would be delivered out the nose of the instrument into a waiting hand. They were given to the workers at the factory my father was a foreman at because of the profuse sweating that occurred while working so closely with giant ovens that fused glass headlamp lenses and there was no way to cool their workspace.

Once the salt pellet came out of the gun I was so afraid I would get caught by my father I ate the evidence. But then the squeezing of the trigger was so much fun, I repeated the steps several times and had to consume those terribly nasty, salty prizes over and over again until I was sick at my stomach.

My mother says I was born with a stomach ache and had one my entire life. Little did she know I was nearly killing my little body with aspirin and bottled elixirs, I can't remember not having stomach trouble.

By the time I was nine, I was diagnosed with an ulcer. Imagine that, a third grader with an ulcer. My mother cut out Cokes and spicy foods and my older sisters were upset that they were not privy to "Thank You" brand apple juice my mother kept in the fridge for me because besides water, it was my only beverage. All I knew was, my first years of life, a lot of the time I felt like crap.

Then the Summer I turned 9, I got my period...

Cinnamon Kugel

This recipe is great for leftover bread. When you want to impress overnight company but don't want to have to spend a lot of money or maybe you just don't have time but you want to feed the masses. I make this for Christmas Morning because you make it the night before and cook it in the morning, less mess and instant goodness!

Ingredients:

10-12 slices of wheat or white bread cut into 2 inch squares
8 eggs (whisked)
1 ½ cups of 2% or Whole milk
2/3 cup of firmly packed brown sugar
¾ stick of butter
Ground cinnamon to sprinkle on top
2 tsp vanilla extract
½ cup of white sugar

1. In a well greased oblong 9x12 glass baking dish, distribute the cut pieces of bread.
2. In a separate mixing bowl, whisk the eggs, milk and vanilla. Set aside.
3. Take the brown sugar and sprinkle over the cut bread, taking time to push the brown sugar bits into the crevices of the bread.
4. Cut the butter into ¼" slices and shove them evenly into the crannies as well. Then top with a heavy sprinkling of ground cinnamon over the entire dish.
5. Pour egg mixture over the entire dish, making sure each bread piece is soaked in the wet mix.
6. Sprinkle white sugar over the top.
7. Cover with Reynolds Wrap and refrigerate overnight.

Next morning, set out 30 minutes before cooking uncovered in a 350* preheated oven. Cook approximately 40 minutes or until fluffy and a knife inserted comes out damp but not sticky. Serve with Maple syrup or Sorghum and a pot or two of great coffee.

Finding Starbucks... a coffee addicts

Pursuit of the Holy Grail
:~:~:~:~:~:~:~:~:~:~:~:~:~:~:

My blood type is Columbian Roast +.

My love for the heavenly coffee bean is definitely an obsession. In fact, I have my coffee maker prepped every night before I go to bed, for the convenience of flipping a switch at 6 am and "Voila!" Five minutes and a packet of Stevia later; hot, steaming, "*coffee crack*".

Few things intimidate me.

Since I entered my 40's, I've faced cancer, surgeries, gray hair and the dreaded teen years with two of my three children, along with being the proud host of a hormone patch, so I find that very little shakes me.

Previously only frivolous feminine venues have made me cower. Victoria's Secret stores and Merle Norman make-up counters were on my short list of things that make me want to stop and run in the opposite direction. But now I can add Starbucks to my little list of intimidators.

My husband recently gave me a gift certificate to Starbucks and even though it has been around for years and years, I have never been to one. So, being the researcher that I am, I felt compelled to type the words, "*How to order a cup of Coffee at Starbucks*" as my Google query and knew I was in trouble when I found there were 618,000 results to choose from. Evidently I was not the only Coffee Kiosk virgin in the world.

I heard friends tell me how much they loved the coffee there, but never could find a reason to buy a 5 dollar cup of java when I could buy nearly a can of my favorite roast and have an entire hot pot at my disposal for an entire morning of writing, cooking, cleaning and "Googling".

When I clicked on my first "how to" I found it listed not one, but SEVEN steps to ordering coffee at Starbucks.

Step 1: <u>Determine the size</u>. Well this seemed simple, I would assume small, medium or large would be my choices, but upon reading further I found that Starbucks has actually invented it's own *Coffee Language*. "Tall, Grande and Venti" were the substitutes and they seemed to have the same meaning. Except for that last one, that's just obnoxious. I was confused, all I wanted was a hot cup of coffee with hazelnut and Stevia.

Step 2:<u>Decaf or Regular</u>. Finally, I knew this lingo. I knew I would be taking mine in it's original high octane form. This was a no- brainer. I actually felt a bit more empowered.

Step 3: <u>Be prepared for milk free coffee</u>. Okay. Mine comes that way. Where have these people been getting their coffee?

Steps 4-6: <u>Specify the 'type" of milk, "how "you like it, and "where" it originates...</u>a city cow, free-range bovine or a soybean. Okay, now its just downright ridiculous. *Low-fat, Whole or Non-fat. Low foam, extra foam, half, chocolate, extra dry,* the list went on and on...I had to keep reading just to see how it would end.

Finally Step 7: <u>Choose your flavoring</u>. Caramel, chocolate, hazelnut or vanilla.

No wonder this calorie free beverage has now become more fattening than a Big Mac and twice as expensive.

Just when I thought I was done with my foot long tutorial I read the disclaimer at the bottom..."*Not all coffee houses have the same language, a coffee you order at your Starbucks may not be the same coffee at another location*" Are they kidding me? All this to find out it really is a toss up anywhere I go? What a waste of my time.

I was determined to use my $10.00 gift certificate and go see exactly what I'd been missing. So I put on my brown corduroy jacket and headed out into the cold, determined to come home with a cup of caffeine that would make my Mr. Coffee coffeemaker cry and hide his shameful face in the corner.

I pulled into the parking lot and took the last available space and sat there for a moment and put on my game face. After all the hype, I was prepared for the Coffee Nazi to take my java rights away if I dared to stutter or repeat myself so I tried to remember what I had learned earlier.

I walked in and found myself not in a rushed high society- "when in doubt, pinkies out" coffeetorium, but instead a room awash in Mom Jeans, lap tops and one male presence texting in the corner.

I admitted to the barista that I didn't know what I was doing. He was non-plussed. I am assuming he gets newbies daily and is just tired of suggesting "exotic" coffees for us stay at home Moms to wash the taste of Chock Full o' Nuts (my favorite coffee) off our tongues.

So he suggested a *"Latte, espresso, blah, blah, blah, with hazelnut, blah, blah, something about foam"* in a Venti, which is Starbucks lingo for large.

What I got for my $4.00 plus change was a nice cup of coffee. Not too hot, not too cold, with a foamy top that resembled hot meringue and a solid coffee flavor with a punch of espresso that would later give me turbo power and then crash me into a near napping stupor while I made dinner. It was delicious. But it seemed almost as if I was sitting at the grown up table at Thanksgiving for the first time. I felt a bit out of place and unworthy of such an inspired and crafted, adult beverage. I missed the comfort of my insulated mug from the dollar store and the knowledge that my daily fat and calorie intake wasn't going to be spent in liquid form.

So I traveled home with my cup made from recycled paper in it's "go-green" cardboard sleeve and sat on the couch and supped upon it with reflection. Turning over the flavor and appreciating the attention to detail that went into my cup.

Then, later that night, I prepped my coffee maker for the next morning, cleaned out the pot and took a bit more time to make sure I had my measurements right, my Stevia supply and plenty of store bought creamer. I placed my insulated mug on stand-by and then quietly and with affection... smiled. For I possessed the knowledge that few do, I had already found my holy grail.

Drunk Raisin Bread (Southern Scones)

Ingredients:

2/3 cup Kentucky Bourbon

1 ½ tsp Vanilla extract

1 Cup Raisins (golden or regular)

6 eggs, separated (yolks in one small dish, whites in another)

1 ¼ C softened butter

1 ½ Cups of granulated sugar

2 ¼ C flour

1 C Pecan pieces (optional)

Soak Raisins in bourbon 3 hours or covered overnight in the fridge. (This plumps them up and they will carry the bourbon throughout your bread and keep them from burning and drying out)

1. Drain raisins but reserve the leftover bourbon liquid.
2. In a bowl, cream the butter and ½ the sugar until fluffy.
3. Add egg yolks, one at a time, beating between each addition.
4. Slowly add flour, stirring as you go and pouring in the bourbon reserve as you need it until it has all blended together. Stir in soaked raisins, vanilla and Pecan pieces.
5. In a separate bowl whisk the egg whites, until stiff. Fold them into the flour mixture. Mix carefully.
6. Grease and flour the bottoms of 2 loaf pans or line with greased wax paper. Pour or spoon in batter.
7. Bake at 350* for 55-65 minutes. This recipe makes two loaves.

The Loud Lullaby...testimony of a Snorer's wife

:~:~:~:~:~:~:~:~:~:~:~:

"What a happy and holy fashion it is that those who love one another should rest on the same pillow". ~Nathaniel Hawthorne

I never would have thought that something as annoying as snoring could find such a sweet spot in my heart. That is, until my husband Dave began leaving for weeklong trips to Indiana and Japan for work and I was left in a bed that was transformed into a sleep deprivation chamber.

I flipped and flopped so much when he first started his journeys, I felt like a human pancake. I finally gave in and just slept with the television on in an attempt to soothe myself into my Melatonin induced shut-eye.

Twenty years.

Over twenty years of snoring. Snoring that started out as a real nuisance. In fact when we first got married, I may have broken a few laws and at the very least a few vows when Dave's "nasal opera" would reach such a fevered pitch that thoughts of smothering my beloved via pillow crossed my mind.

However, I learned to adapt without killing him and devised a pretty sneaky technique in my sleep bankrupt state that would cause him to wake up and turn over...

Let's just put it this way, it involved two fingers and cutting off air supply to his nose. After the application of *"said technique"*, he would levitate from his pillow and let out a small gasp for air. I would pretend to wake up from his flailing about and whisper nicely while reaching out a hand for comfort..."*Honey are you okay*?" To which he would utter a small grunt or groan and change position.

Due to his new adjustment and turn to the other side of the mattress, it allowed me a few moments of quiet time to slip into my much needed coma.

It may sound avaricious, but in reality I was quite gentle and it's much nicer than a jab to the ribs and let's face it, lack of rest could have lead me to do much worse over the span of twenty years without a few decent winks while raising three children through their first fretful months of life.

But now, I no longer find his snoring to be an issue. In fact, it has become a lullaby of love. His interminable snoring is a reminder that he is there next to me in the dark. It has become the soundtrack for my slumber and it puts a smile on my face when I turn over and hear logs being sawed in repetition through the night.

It's odd how the things in life that you think are aggravating, turn out to be endearing as you age. Now, we both laugh about my midnight snuffing of the "*zzzzzz's*". It took a few years for me to confess how I handled his snoring, but when I did tell him, he just looked at me and laughed. I think he knew about it anyway and now it's a running joke among our family and friends.

I have to admit Dave's patience with me is amazing. I definitely married "up", because as far as I know he has yet to jeopardize my life during R.E.M., but a lot could happen over the next twenty years.

"Too Tired Tater Tot Casserole"

Maybe you were up all night and couldn't sleep, maybe you just are worn out from the work week...regardless dinner time is here and you need to feed your family. Here's a quick recipe that the kids will enjoy and you have little to clean up when you're done.

Ingredients:
1 bag frozen Tater Tots
1 lb. ground beef
1 can cream of mushroom soup
1 pkg. Shredded yellow cheese (Colby or cheddar)
1 onion (chopped)
1 green pepper (chopped)
Salt and pepper

1. Brown ground beef in a skillet with onion and green pepper. Drain the grease.
2. Add Mushroom soup and stir.
3. Add 1 tsp salt and 1 tsp pepper.
4. Pour into greased casserole dish.
5. Top with Tater tots sprinkle on cheese.
6. Bake 20 minutes at 375*, call the kids and fetch the ketchup!

(For extra zing, add a few drops of hot sauce to your ketchup)

Mama's lessons
:~:~:~:~:~:~:~:~:~:~:

As I mentioned before, when I was young my Mama didn't work outside the home. We spent our entire days together. For some reason she didn't drive, never had a desire to get behind the wheel after my sisters and I were born. This would drive me crazy now, but somehow she managed to keep her sanity and we all survived. I'm assuming some sort of relaxant made its way into our home, either that or she was a Saint because I don't ever remember her drinking, but I do know that our local pharmacy on Southland drive delivered.

After she finished her black coffee at our house or at a neighbor's, she and I would go through our entire day together, side by side.

When she ironed, I ironed.

At age 4, I had my own ironing board, and a small pink iron that really worked. Mama would do the large things, and I always ironed my father's handkerchiefs. They were always fresh from the clothes line. I had to give them a whiff before I started my ironing just to take in the outdoors. Every one of them was different. Some had a little crocheted edge, some had embroidery and occasionally Daddy would have an initial monogrammed on one of his hankies. If I ran out of hankies, I would iron pillowcases. My Mother ironed everything. She had a glass coke bottle with a few holes hammered through the lid for sprinkling water on shirts for steam ironing. We weren't big on spray starch.

Sometimes we would iron for what seemed like hours. Sometimes we just talked, other times she would turn on her little black and white TV and we would watch a game show or General Hospital. When we weren't ironing, we were sorting clothes, and hanging them out on the line to dry.

My needs seemed so much simpler then. My desire to eat constantly was non existent. For the most part, I lived a full and hunger satisfied life as a child. Lunch was usually a grilled cheese or Peanut Butter and

Jelly. Occasionally, if Mama was all caught up on her work and the weather was right, lunch might be a small teddy bear picnic on the hot concrete porch complete with a real Coke in my own glass bottle.

For some reason, I always liked my Cokes room temperature. I believed it made it fizzier.

At some point during the day we had to get ready for Supper. This usually meant going to the basement and finding a meat from our huge freezer. Usually, deer roasts or steaks for the next day were brought up to thaw. Our freezer was always packed with crappie, bluegill, deer, homemade sausage and just about any other meat that was available. I never knew what a finicky eater was. We always had good food, even if it was liver and onions, my mother made it melt in your mouth.

Because she felt that taking care of the house was her job, she did it very well, she had a schedule with breaks that included her friends, but her house ran like a clock and dinner was always ready everyday when my Dad got home or very close to it. Our home may not have been spotless, but it was close. She had my sisters clean on Saturday mornings and it lasted nearly all week. Mama managed to maintain a complicated beehive hairdo all week too. I have to wash mine at least once a day. If I'm going out later in the evening, I take another shower, but my Mama managed to keep that coif in place all day, even tape her side curls in place at night and wear a scarf to hold it all together.

Life was so much simpler then. There weren't many things going on. Kids didn't really have that many outside interests like organized sports or clubs. We just played in the yard or rode bikes. TV wasn't a priority like it is now. As kids, we did our own thing every afternoon, from red light/green light to hide-n-seek, we played until we couldn't see one another in the dark or until someone's mother called them in for the night.

We hear terms like Super Mom and give that title to the women of today, but honestly, we have it easy. In my mothers day eating out happened maybe once a week, and that was if you were lucky. Meals were made everyday and pennies were counted for everything. No credit cards or cash-in-advance, they had to make the money last and they did. I don't ever remember missing a meal.

We didn't have a lot of snacks but we did have Fig Newton's and a Coke now and then. But mostly we had bananas, raisins and crackers. Sometimes for a late night snack we would take a glass of ice cold milk and crumble corn bread in it and eat it with a spoon, I read somewhere that it was called a "country Milkshake" but I just prefer the term Milk Soup. It was good, and it was filling and it cost about 4 cents.

Mama fried a mean chicken and even snuck in frog legs once and we all loved 'em. She could take any type of meat and make it great, she learned how to soak the "game-i-ness" out of meats ranging from Buffalo to Moose with buttermilk. She would take the tiny grouse breasts and fry them up to perfection. No one could hold a candle to the home maker that my Mama was. Once my mama said she felt sorry for those little Grouse, so much work to bread them and fry them up only to end up the size of a chicken liver. She said it was a waste to shoot such small creatures.

When I reached high school, Mama started showing signs of illness. Doctors thought at first she had Lupus. After more testing they told her she had Rheumatoid arthritis and it was advancing quickly. She had gold shots, drank aloe vera juice, she did diets that limited certain foods and it still progressed daily. There weren't a lot of medications available at that time and she relied on aspirin and Motrin for most of her pain. Since then, my mother has had knee and shoulder replacements along with a ligament replacement in one of her hands and a pacemaker. She is our bionic Mama. She has had such a difficult time with her Arthritis and I don't see how she does it. She rarely makes it into the kitchen anymore. My father has had to do most of the cooking.

Now she wears her pain like an apron. I know that it is difficult to get up in the morning, but she does, most days she gets dressed to her shoes and always looks nice. The lessons I learned with my mother are still ones I use today, even though I only get my ironing board out for Sunday clothes, and I prefer cream and sugar in my coffee.

She taught me how to run my home like a job. She showed me that just being at home wasn't enough, that people rely on me to do my part and that we all have responsibilities even as children and even if they are hard. I'm not ashamed or afraid to admit I am a housewife. It's a full time job that doesn't pay in cash, but it does have it's rewards. I don't think I could ever be as good a Mama to my kids as she was to me, or keep my house as clean. I freely admit it, I feel like I am ready to scream by 8:00 on some nights as I shuffle my own monkeys into their rooms for my own sanity.

But there are times, when it is peaceful and lovely.

Like when I read a book with my youngest in the big chair and we both drift off for a nap and when we wake up, she helps me fold wash cloths "her way".

That's when I get a craving deep inside for a teddy bear picnic, Fig Newton's and a room-temp Coke-a-Cola.

Watergate Salad

This is an oldie, even for me, but I bet your Mama or Grandma may recall this one. I remember this being made when I was too young to even know what Watergate even meant. I do know that it is delicious and it was really popular when I was a child and when else will you have an occasion to use Pistachio pudding?

Ingredients:
    1- 20 oz can of crushed pineapple (with juice)
    1- pkg instant pistachio pudding
    1 Cup miniature marshmallows
    ½ Cup Crushed or finely chopped pecan pieces
    1- 9 oz container of Cool Whip or non-dairy topping

Mix all ingredients together and set overnight in refrigerator. Flavor improves after setting.

This recipe is great for potlucks, cookouts or game nights when you need a side dish that isn't too sweet.

Lunch Lady Love
:~:~:~:~:~:~:~:~:~:~:

"We are living in a world today where lemonade is made from artificial flavors and furniture polish is made from real lemons."
~Alfred E. Newman

They would arrive at school just minutes after we settled into our desks. I remember seeing them pull up behind our elementary school, disembarking from their station wagons, Chevette's and Volkswagen mini buses...those wonderful, blue haired, angels frocked in homemade rick-rack aprons with hand-stitched front pockets and ready to join the ranks of their fellow lunch ladies in the cafeteria kitchen. Most likely, each of these *Warriors of the cookery* was an accomplished cook in their own rite.

By 10:00 the heavenly smells would begin to waft through the corridors of Clays Mill elementary carrying scents of freshly baked Sally Lunn bread, Salisbury steaks and green beans with ham. In our school, magic was at work in the kitchen. Dishes were being prepared from scratch and breads were made as we studied quietly at our little individual desks silently salivating. We knew that our forty-five cent lunch was going to be worth its weight in gold.

What has happened to the school lunch of my youth? Processed foods have taken over the lunch tray. Try and find an actual piece of chicken on a plate, you won't. It's all shaped, processed and filled with breading and fillers. You can't even find chicken on a bone. Everything is cheesed-up, dipped-up and package-gravied-up. To me, it all resembles carnival food and its mouth watering color is charming, monotone beige. In fact, according to the school lunch menu I was given at the beginning of the year for my own kids, everyday there is some form of processed chicken product. In the form of stix, nuggets, sandwiches, baskets, dippers, flower petals or popcorn shapes.

What happened to grilled cheese and tomato soup? Salisbury steak, baked chicken and baked spaghetti? It's all been replaced with prepackaged, frozen, processed foods that arrive in trays and are warmed in microwave ovens for the kids to eat.

Its no wonder obesity is on the rise, with so many fillers, extra calories and lack of good solid nutrition and whole foods in our school lunches. You can't tell me it's cheaper to give processed chicken nuggets than it is to serve a good ole baked chicken leg.

I don't understand why we are taking the easy way out in food preparation for our kids and then complaining that Billy Jo is wearing 42 inch waist Men's Wranglers in 3rd grade. Kids need two major things that are quickly being reduced in our schools, outdoor play and adequate time to eat a nutritious meal that should be based on a whole foods theme and not on a scale of whether the kids think the food is "fun" or not. Flower petal chicken, Pizza dippers, stuffed crust pizza, chicken nuggets, these foods are fast foods. I never ate any of these at my elementary school and we were all fit as a fiddle.

Although I am sure the frozen food supplier for our country's school systems are elated to have this opportunity, I just don't see how it benefits our children nutritionally. What I do know is, the school lunch they have now is nothing compared to the school lunch I had as a child and money was just as hard to come by then as it is now. I don't even want to hear about how costly good food is, I know for a fact it is more expensive to take my kids to McDonalds than to make a good homemade nutritious meal and even then, we have leftovers we can use for a future meal.

Plus, we are talking about our children, are they not worthy of a good lunch? So much emphasis is placed on technology in the classroom. *Techy* gadgets and computers are always sought after through fundraisers. If I buy another scented candle on behalf of furthering the technological agenda at school I will have enough to light up the neighborhood like an Amish Las Vegas.

But where is the rally for whole foods? In my own town, just the mention of this issue through our local newspaper brought me hate mail, emails and letters to the Editor from a few angered cafeteria workers with their hairnets tied up in a cranky ol' knot. I struck a nerve with some of them and it had me wondering if they were going to petition to serve cotton candy and funnel cakes with their "Carny food" just to show me that they could. One even went into a rant that their "processed chicken product" had "real whole grain breading". How yummy, "Chicken Product" with "genuine" breading. My mouth was definitely watering, but not because of hunger.

But on the positive side I also got feedback from other cafeteria personnel, parents and teachers that supported my query into the nutritional value of the new school lunch.

I pack my children's lunch. All three. My oldest son has already requested I make his lunch for college. On average it costs me about 1.45 per child or less. They take soup in thermoses, crackers and cheese, a fruit and drink. Sometimes they have a sandwich, Jell-o and banana and baked chips or if the pantry is low, a baggie of dry cereal will work as the "crunch" factor. Unfortunately, not all parents can make school lunch though, some of them are either too busy or have left for work before their kids leave for school. I make lunch ahead of time and put it in the fridge the night before if it isn't in a thermos, but you can make a sandwich, drink, fruit and chips and have it ready to go in the a.m. if you just set aside 5 minutes before bed.

I used to think that by having my kids purchase the school lunch it would put a nice hot meal in their tummies. I thought this until I went to school and watched as Lydia and the other kids in her class picked at their trays and threw most of their lunches away. I realized then why she was so tired and fussy at the end of the day. She was still hungry after her lunch tray of *bland, limp and blah..*

I think we need to seriously ask ourselves where the classic school lunch has gone. Where has the "blue-haired happy grandma" gone? I miss her. She greeted me every day in school as she ladled up soup or spaghetti onto my sky blue food tray and cut me a slice of homemade yeast bread with a pat of real butter on a small white paper square. She made me healthy, happy and content so I could concentrate the rest of the day and not have to listen to a rumbly tummy.

School age kids need unprocessed food, good cooks and a full and pleasant 30 minutes to enjoy lunch again. Although school work is important, so is good nutrition and I just don't see it inside a processed chicken strip, whatever the shape.

Baked Chicken with Bones!

Alert the media and notify the children, there will be no "processed chicken product" served in my house. When chicken is so versatile and easy, why settle for formed and mechanically separated poultry refuse? Dig in, buy fresh and in the famous words of my Granny Miller, *"Take out and eat!"*

Ingredients:
2 to 3 lbs of chicken on the bone.
1 stick of butter (REAL butter please)
Juice of 1 lemon
4 Tbs of Worcestershire sauce
Salt and pepper to taste
Boiling water
Small dish of flour

1. Wash the chicken pieces and then salt them as desired.
2. Dust them generously with a dredge through the flour.
3. Place the floured chicken in a baking dish, (pieces not touching)
4. Pour lemon juice and Worcestershire in a bowl and blend with 1 and 1/2 cups of boiling water.
5. Pour **around** the chicken pieces not over them and then dot the floured chicken with cut stick butter slices.
6. Bake at 350* for 1 and ½ hours. Baste occasionally if necessary.

Serve with rice blends, mashed potatoes and/or steamed broccoli.

The Bible School Junkie
:~:~:~:~:~:~:~:~:~:~:~:

"Childhood is a short season." ~Helen Hayes

When I was young, I loved my Summers. Not only for the playtime outside, late mornings and the absence of school, but I loved going to Bible School. Its odd but I never went to the bible school at my own church, maybe because my mother didn't drive so we relied on the kindness of my Aunt and neighbors who didn't mind if I tagged along to their churches.

My family and I are Southern Baptists so exploring other churches and their traditions, even if they were very similar was very interesting to me. I would attend my cousins Christian church located in downtown Lexington for morning bible school, where we would play, make friends, learn a Bible story and then do a craft.

I loved craft time at Bible School the most. I made potholders, tissue paper flowers, cookbook stands, letter holders and a plethora of plaster o' Paris doodads that read *"Home Sweet Home"* and *"Smile God Loves You"*. My mother would proudly display my artwork in the living room for a week or so and then retire my pieces to my bedroom and finally a box in the attic. However, she would use the letter and recipe holders until they would eventually break. She was always so proud of my Bible school endeavors.

After morning Bible school, my aunt Louise would drive us home to her house and we would have lunch. Lunch would consist of, half a tuna salad sandwich, Kool-aid and Charles Chips from the giant speckled yellow and brown metal tin.

My cousins and I would play until dinner time and then Aunt Louise would take me back home exhausted after my full day of Bible learnin', crafts and cousins. I don't know what I would have done without my Aunt Louise. We all have those special people in our lives that manage to get us where we need to go, find what we need or be there for us even when we don't realize we need them. That was Aunt "Weezy". She would come and get me and take me to her house on days when I thought I might lose my mind if I stayed inside or home one more second without traveling in a car somewhere. Anywhere.

For one or two weeks in the Summer I would attend my neighbor Carol's, Assembly of God church. My next door neighbor Carol was my best friend. She had two sisters like I did, but they were closer to her age. Their church, The First Assembly of God, was just up the road from our house so we would usually walk unless we were running behind or if it was raining and then we would all pile into their sky blue Volkswagen station wagon. This was before mandatory seatbelts so all four of us girls would try to cram into the rear storage area for the 3 minute ride.

The Assembly church was probably my favorite for Bible school. Their property was right next to the small farm across the street from my house, where my older sisters took me a few times for pony rides. The church had a barn they used for crafts and I just loved being in there, I love the smell and the feeling of all things farm-like. I always have.

There is just something very comforting about the smell of hay and sweet feed to me. We would start out in the basement of the church, study the bible, separate into groups to memorize a verse, have snack, play dodge ball or volleyball outside and then do a craft at the end of the night. By the end of the week they would hold a graduation and we would all get a small trophy. I loved those trophies. I would say by the time I turned 12, I had at least 6 or more in my collection.

My sisters called me the "Bible School junkie". If anyone invited me, I would go. I loved getting out of the house and meeting people, trying on new customs and just exploring. The first time I saw a woman speaking in tongues at my friend Carol's church I was terrified. Then, as the years progressed I just accepted that there would be the occasional member at the Assembly church stand and begin to speak in a language I couldn't understand. I realized it had nothing to do with me and it didn't matter if she got loud or babbled on too long, nobody else seemed impressed either.

Once I reached junior high school my bible school days had come to an end. I missed them, my Summers even seemed less fulfilling without my crafts, bible verses and tiny plastic trophies and evening snack of generic Oreos and juice.

Bible school days were gone for years, but now that I have three kids of my own, as soon as they were able, I had them signed up and attending at least two bible schools each Summer. They have been to Assembly, Christian, our own Baptist church and other Baptist's at least once each and our youngest child, Lydia has attended Bible school the past four Summers at the church near our neighborhood.

Lydia seems to love her bible school time as much as I did when I was young. It makes my heart glad, just knowing how much fun she is having, what wonderful people she is with and what great lessons she is learning. It looks like I may have ended up with a little "Bible School junkie' of my own; and I sure could use a *"Home Sweet Home"* recipe holder.

Mushroom Baptized Chicken Pot Pie

I'm not sure what we did before Cream of Mushroom soup was available, but I am assuming there were a lot of dry pork chops and tasteless casseroles being consumed nationwide.
Pot pie soothes the savage beast and warms the belly. Chicken pot pie is a great way to say I love you. Nothing can take the place of a hug, but chicken pot pie sure comes close.

Ingredients:
4-6 chicken breasts or one whole chicken.
(Cooked, deboned, diced.)
1 can cream of mushroom soup
1 can cream of chicken soup
1 bag of frozen mixed vegetables (thawed)
1 cup of shredded cheddar cheese

1. Preheat oven to 350*
2. Mix ingredients together in a large bowl.
3. Pour into greased glass dish
4. top with crust:

Easy Crust: Unroll one package of Crescent roll dough and roll lightly with a rolling pin on a floured surface. Slice in strips if you are eager and want to attempt a lattice top for your pie or
Just simply place rolled dough as a sheet over top of your pie filling and make slices to vent crust. Bake until brown and bubbly.

"How I killed my first Hot Dog"
:~:~:~:~:~:~:~:~:~:~:~:~:~:~:

Like most new-age Mama's, I was using my microwave one morning to make a 29 second breakfast of leftover pancakes for my kids and I thought about how often I use that magical contraption and how difficult my life would be to give it up.

What would I do if I had to actually take the time to make everything on the stove? Popcorn made in a pan? The mere thought was sacrilege. Could Mr. Redenbacher continue his monopoly on popcorn without my patronage? Where would that time come from to wait for kernels to heat over a burner? What would I give up, seeing as my day was a constant "to do" list I could only imagine that I would have to give up showering, stop sleeping or both.

I rely on my microwave way more than I ever realized I would. How this small appliance become such a necessity in my life I have no idea, because my parents never wanted one to begin with- in fact when I first used a microwave I was fifteen years old and I can still remember the smell of our first carbonized creation...

The year was 1979, I was a junior in high school, and everyone else on the planet had cable television and a microwave oven but the "Millers". Knowing that my parent's would never go for cable TV, I began to campaign for the microwave. Just the thought of my friends coming over and having to wait for the conventional oven to warm up to pop in some frozen snacks would move me down the rungs on an already teetering ladder of popularity. My parents were the age of everyone else's grandparents…almost so for just about everything I planned on doing required at the very least a small crusade to accomplish.

"I will never have one of those things, in my house. They probably cause cancer", my Father had told me after I asked him for the microwave the first time.

I placed ads for them near my fathers chair, remarked about how much easier it made the lives of my friends mothers to my Mom, how great things would taste and how we really needed to get on board and move into the 21st century with the rest of the world, but I knew if I pushed it too much they would balk and we would be pushed back to the stone age and I could very well end up with my father purchasing a wood burning stove just to prove a point with me chopping wood every afternoon, instead of joy riding with my friends. So I had to be careful. My father was of the "my way or the highway" generation.

Then one day out of the blue the impossible happened. I came home from school and there it was in all it's glory...A HUGE microwave perched precariously on the counter top. It was by all accounts the Goliath of microwaves. Nearly as big as our conventional oven. Because my father, is a *go big or go home* fella, I should have known he would purchase one so large that it had to sit catty-cornered on the counter just to fit.

I marveled at the buttons, the modernistic tinted windows and the way the numbers illuminated in their little window...I was in shock.

"What would you like to cook first?" my Mama asked. I thought about it, searched my mind for the ultimate culinary delight a la microwave...and a plump juicy hot dog came to mind, that type that would taste like it came straight from the ballpark. My mouth was already watering.

Keeping with family tradition, we skipped the directions that lay untouched in the appliance box and unwrapped an Oscar Mayer wiener. We put that little fella on a plate in the center of the microwave arena. We discussed briefly a guess at a cook time and then came to the conclusion to set the timer on HI for three minutes.

The *hummmm* of the microwave sounded like a lullaby, we watched in awe as our hot dog began to cook before our eyes. At first, it made only a few popping sounds and *we gasped*. It began to plump up into the most beautiful vision of perfection we had ever imagined, and *we actually clapped*. As time passed, the third minute seemed to change the hot dog, actually mutate it into something I've never seen in any food group. Then the tiny bell rang, "DING!" and our pork dirigible that had swollen to the size of a small loaf of bread began to deflate, and *we roared*.

What lay before us was an abomination. What had only seconds earlier been a vision of a perfectly plump pork balloon of tastiness, that had nearly brought me to tears with anticipation, had sizzled into a bright pink strip of Slim Jim or better yet, a twig from the apple tree.

Through the awkward silence, Mama turned and looked me straight in the eye and said *"I think we bought a jerky maker by mistake."* I laughed 'til I nearly peed my pants.

Now being a girl raised by a hunter, I'll try anything. I've eaten a little bit of any critter that is big enough to catch a bullet or a hook. But I had to draw the line at this particular strip of protein. We didn't even offer it to the dog.

The heat that radiated from that strip of pork and nitrates was remarkable. I think it actually continued to cook after the power was off. It had become Magma. That poor hot dog is probably still hot 60 feet below in the landfill. It may in fact, be responsible for global warming.

After her introduction to the world of nuclear scorching, my Mama immediately signed up for Microwave Cooking classes with our neighbor at the local Adult Education center one night a week.

Week #1:
Defrosting.

The first week at Microwave Wizardry taught eager students how to defrost meats and poultry. In no time, Mama was fetching out gray pounds of ground beef, hot on the outside and frozen solid in the center, along with chicken breasts that were sizzling white on the edges and a cool fleshy pink on top. My father wasn't impressed and I was beginning to wish I hadn't instigated the idea for this culinary contraption in the house. I just wanted something to warm up cold pizza. This was getting tedious and disappointing.

Week #2:
Baked Potatoes.

The lesson also included what NOT to microwave, like foil, whole eggs and Styrofoam. Did you know eggs explode? They also smell like sewage if they are overcooked. Coincidentally, I had already found all of this valuable information via my own testing facility at home.

By week number 3 and 4....Mom was pre-cooking veggies for broccoli casseroles with aplomb and frying bacon on tiny special plates she bought at cooking class. She was trying out new recipes from her new 20 dollar hardback cookbook and making every effort to convince my father that the meatloaf was DONE though it was gray and slightly plastic in appearance. She tried really hard, but it was impossible to cut with a knife and the texture resembled the sturdy foam of a couch cushion.

Thank the Lord...there was no week number five.

Over that four week period we all realized that we missed Mom's old ways. We missed browned meats and potatoes wrapped in foil, bacon that didn't have paper towel stuck to one side and scrambled eggs that didn't smell like stink bombs. Maybe waiting for a meal was worth it, maybe faster wasn't better.

So, it was back to the conventional oven for my Mother. Her attempts at new age cooking had not met with the approval she had hoped for. I was majorly disappointed. We were all elated when we heard the *jiggle-jiggle* of the pressure cooker that used to keep us out of the kitchen in fear of an explosion resulting in loss of limbs. The pull start fan over the stove carrying out the heavenly smells of foods cooked for hours in roasting pans had our mouths watering once again.

The weeks with the microwave had slightly altered and scalded our taste buds. We were all thankful that Mom had turned away from her microwave education.

But for me, I'm finally learning to defrost meats in the microwave, I'm also learning that there is more than one temperature setting.

However, I'll never trust it for meatloaf.

I still make bacon sometimes that has napkin tattoos, and I've even caught a few things on fire during my nuking test flights. But I persist to save time.

Just like when I was a kid, my own children's eyes light up when they see me get out the pressure cooker or the crock pot, because they have learned just like I did, that quicker isn't always better. They have a great appreciation of good food and waiting is sometimes hard, but the sweet reward is worth the wait.

Over the years, my parents have won three microwaves in giveaways and raffles. They have given me two, and my sister one. They haven't kept any because they are convinced their first one still works fine. It reheats a cup of coffee, it can warm up a slice of coffee cake, and on occasion it can cook a fine hot dog as long as you keep an eye on it.

And now... a moment of silence for our flame-kissed fallen hero, the hot dog that *didn't* come to dinner.

Microwave Applesauce Coconut Bars

Ingredients:

Filling:
1 TBS lemon juice
1 ½ Cup applesauce
¼ Cup Dark brown sugar (packed)
2 TBS flour
Bottom:
½ Cup butter
½ Cup Dark Brown Sugar (packed)
½ Cup flour
1 Cup quick cooking oatmeal
Topping:
½ Tsp cinnamon
½ Cup shredded coconut

1. Combine applesauce, ¼ cup dark brown sugar, 2 TBS flour and lemon juice in a 1 quart casserole. (first 4 ingredients)
2. Microwave on full power for 2 ½ - 3 minutes or until thick and bubbly. Cool.
3. Cream butter and ½ cup of brown sugar. Blend in flour and oats. Press mixture against bottom of a 8x8x2" glass dish. Microwave on full power for 2 ½ minutes. Let cool 5 minutes.
4. Spread cooled applesauce mixture (first 4 ingredients) over bottom layer. Mix cinnamon and coconut. Sprinkle over applesauce. Microwave on full power for 5-6 minutes or until filling is bubbly and begins to pull away from sides of the dish. CHILL. Cut into bars. Makes 16 bars.

Thank God for Baby Wipes

:~:~:~:~:~:~:~:~:~:~:~:~:~:

I love baby wipes. How do people get by without 'em? None of my children are in diapers and I still buy them. Yep, you can find me slinking my way over to the "baby aisle" at Kroger's slipping a box of cheap baby wipes into my cart at least once a month. I feel like a cheat, like I'm sneaking into the movies from the back door. I know parents of newborns sense my deceit. They know I don't belong in their club. My hair is done, I look rested and I don't have any dried food in my hair or on my shoulder from burping a wee one.

I'm a 'tween myself, I just passed my childbearing years, but I've not quite entered the adult diaper stage.

I look like an outsider to the walking dead that linger there. They stand hump shouldered, researching baby formula labels, trying to look like they slept a full eight while wearing the same clothes they wore yesterday and maybe the day before. I try not to show my pity.

I used to look down the baby aisle and think maybe I needed one more mouth to feed. I could imagine taking on a newborn. Then reality would sink in when one of the Kroger Babies would begin to cry at 900 decibels from their cave-like quarters atop the shopping carts. This wailing opera would force me to quickly re-evaluate my stand on sleepless nights and vomit covered Lee jeans. In fact, once I had my hysterectomy, that biological clock I had to keep resetting, finally ran out of batteries altogether. I feel like I've done my stint as *baby mama*...time to move on to the next phase, whatever that is.

I am Al Gores nightmare, I don't leave a carbon footprint, I leave a full body chalk outline. I love microwave popcorn, instant grits, Lunchables, dryer sheets, Swiffers, toss out toilet brush heads, jell-O cups, Tide pens and Spam.

With all these modern conveniences, how do I still not have any time on my hands?

Lately, I have heard from all three of my kids that I am always *busy*. Of course, I have three kids making messes and adding to the laundry pile that need to be fed and cleaned on a regular basis, but I still can't figure out where my time is going. I assigned "duties" for each of the kids, which really helps, but we still run out of daylight. I miss having time to do nothing. With homework, studying, projects and bathing we are going 50 miles an hour, five days a week and we are missing our time to unwind.

Now that I am getting older, I think about my youth a lot. I miss those lazy days where the sun never seemed to set. I miss waking up energized, racing to find my shoes, slipping down the stairs for a quick bowl of instant apples n' cinnamon oatmeal before running out the door to my friends house with the screen door banging shut behind me.

Sometimes, on a summer morning when I would run to my neighbor Carol's back porch to see if she could play, the milkman had just made his delivery. I could see the sweat forming on the top of their aluminum milk keeper on the back porch. Fascinated, I always had to take a peak inside. Same order every time; Cottage cheese and 2 quarts of moo juice.

My friend Carol and I would play outside for hours. When we went *"out"* to play, that is what we did. We didn't have much equipment except a metal swing set that pitched one leg out of the ground every time you went too high, squirt guns, baby dolls, banana seat bikes, two badminton racquets and a few lopsided Frisbees. We were even entrusted with Lawn *J'arts*. For those of you that may not know what these were, they were large heavy darts that you flung into hula hooped shaped targets on the ground about twenty feet apart; however it was rare to see kids use them properly. We would take the heavy lawn darts and throw them straight up in the air and then run...turning just in time to see them thrust their weighty points 2-3 inches into the hard earth. Yes, they were dangerous and yes, there were fatalities from their use...mostly kids. All kids playing with them incorrectly; just like us. But we were spared any injuries and within a few years they were discontinued. But our parents allowed us to play with them until they were lost or destroyed...they really were cool.

We made real mud pies, in the plastic lids of coffee cans and dried them in the sun. Some were fancy, with the bright yellow heads of dandelions on top, or grass blended in for texture, but they were all beautiful. Easy to clean up, just pop their dried disc shaped bodies out behind the Forsythia bush and make some more.

Everybody's yard was fenced in. Each house had a dog or a child, or both. We played kickball, red light/green light, badminton and tag. A new 50 cent kickball from K-Mart bouncing on the blacktop was like *the call of the wild* for the kids in our neighborhood. That glorious plastic ball swirled with colors of white, green and pink was a vision of beauty. It was sad when the first black streaks appeared on the surface from the driveway. In a matter of weeks, that tightly blown ball would deflate, fade and disappear, and someone else would arrive with a replacement from the TG&Y or K-Mart.

These days, we live in such a fast paced, hurried, dangerous and cautious world. My mother could turn me out for the day and we could run up and down the street from house to house unchaperoned. Now I find myself watching my children walk to a friends house worried they will be abducted or harassed, and we live in a very safe neighborhood.

I am sad for my kids that they will never know the freedom that I had as a child. I remember days when I only showed up when my mother called me in for dinner. I grew up in central Kentucky, about 25 miles from where we live now. My hometown was quiet then and not the big city it is today. When our ball rolled into the street, a quick look right and left and we could retrieve it. Now the street I grew up on is like a highway.

It definitely was a simpler time, we had simpler needs. Kids seemed happy. We had a bit of homework, but not much. Most studies were done during the school day. We didn't have many take home projects, state and government testing was limited, and I consider myself a fairly intelligent person in spite of our shortened work load. Kids need the enjoyment of a life less rushed and complicated.

I hope our children have memories as simple as how precious a new ball can be. They deserve that, a time that they can embrace.

I am going to save those coffee can lids from my Chock Full O' Nuts for the Spring, when the mud is plenty, and teach my little one the art of pie making, and when we're done, I can use those baby wipes I'm so fond of, to clean her up.

Chocolate Chip Pie

Keep those wipes handy when you make this pie. It's a bit sticky, delicious and oh so sinful. Why it's so good...*it'll make you slap your Grandmaw.*

Ingredients:

1 Cup of sugar
½ Cup of flour
2 eggs, beaten
1 stick of butter, softened
1 Cup of English Walnuts, (broken)
1 pkg Chocolate chips
1 tsp Vanilla

1. Mix Sugar and Flour.
2. Then add eggs, butter, walnuts, chocolate chips and vanilla.
3. Pour in unbaked pie shell.
4. Bake at 325* for one hour.
5. Great a la mode with vanilla ice cream or whipped cream.

Me and the Big ol' Boy;
My Iron Skillet love affair
:~:~:~:~:~:~:~:~:~:~:~:~:

If you don't own one, you have no idea what I'm talkin' about. But I love my big ol' iron skillet.

I have several small ones my Daddy gave me that belonged to my Granny, a corn stick pan from my Mama as well as a 45-pound Dutch oven, but my favorite has to be the *"Big ol' boy."*

Big ol' Boy is the one that nearly breaks my wrists when I heave it onto my ceramic cook-top or retrieve it, hot as a fire poker, from the oven. It takes a lot of work to turn a chunk of shiny cast iron that initially destroys all food into something that may look like it was hammered and tempered in the flames of hell but will treat a sunny-side-up egg like the fragile beauty that it is. He is, now and forever more, my gentle giant.

It took me a while to appreciate the joys of iron skillet cooking. My husband, Dave, was actually the one who purchased Big Boy at a discount store. I told him he was crazy. *"That thing is too heavy, it's gonna break my arms off."* I told him when he put it in our shopping cart and it broke the front axle. What was he thinking? I went on to tell him that they now made nonstick gems that were nearly weightless and made eggs come off with just a "Ta-DA!" and gave the air a flourish with my invisible spatula.

He assured me that over time, I would like it. It would take lots of "seasoning," but eventually it would be great.

That was about 15 years ago. For what seemed like years, every time the oven was on, Dave would slip that big skillet in there with a little oil or shortening in it or cook it up if the oven was still warm. We'd try the occasional egg in it, only to find that it would take 10 eggs to make one we could scrape from the top of the nine-egg layer of crust and dehydrated egg-dust adhering to the pan.

Then, one day, it happened. I put in a dozen eggs to scramble and nearly a dozen came out.

And they were delicious.

There is something about an iron skillet that actually "adds" flavor to food. Every meal made in it before, sucks the flavors and delicious hints of each mouthwatering morsel and infuses that into whatever is cooking. It sounds silly, but I read somewhere that iron skillets actually may add iron to your food. They are healthier for you than pans with spray-on finishes or aluminum, and when some of those fancy nonstick pans get too hot, they leech out a toxic fume.

No, thanks, I've got enough issues; I'll stick with my "Little House on the Prairie"-inspired cookware.

Now after some practice, I can cook anything in them; Cornbread, rice, sausage skillet suppers and even solitary eggs or omelets. But never, and I repeat never, put them in the dishwasher or all your hard work is gone and it could raise your spouse's blood pressure and make them cry.

I learned this the hard way. I did it not only once, but twice to a small set we were adding to our 700-pound cookware set. Dave was not happy.

But he forgave me and before I knew it, to make amends I was tossing those little pans in with Big Boy when he was in the oven. Before long we had a happy iron family nesting in the now-broken oven drawer.

I think I'm a lot like my big iron skillet. Way too heavy, I look worn, weathered and if you catch me in the morning, before my coffee, like I was tempered in the flames of hell. It doesn't take a lot to release things from my surface and I'm definitely better seasoned than any newfangled non-stick models.

Although if I do get too hot; I've been known to leech a few toxins.

Pineapple Upside Down Cake a la' Big Ol' Boy

Ingredients:
1 Pineapple cake mix
1 Can crushed pineapple in juice (drain and reserve juice)
2 cups of firmly packed brown sugar
1 stick of butter
Pinch of salt

1. Preheat oven to 375* (or cake mix directed temperature)

2. In a large deep greased Iron skillet on the stovetop, simmer and stir butter, drained pineapple, brown sugar and salt on Medium. Cook until thickened and stir often. (about 4 minutes) Remove from heat. Spread cooked mixture evenly across bottom of skillet.

3. In a bowl, prepare cake mix as directed but use reserved pineapple juice for the water measurement. (Add water to the reserved juice to equal required measured water ingredient for mix).

4. Pour over heated pineapple topping in skillet. Do not stir. Do not overfill.

5. Place in oven and cook according to cake mix directions. Cake is done when knife inserted in center 1 inch comes out clean.

6. When cake is done. Loosen cake with knife from side of skillet. Invert skillet onto cake plate. Allow cake and pineapple topping to release and fall onto inverted plate. This could take a few minutes. Remove skillet and behold, delicious pineapple upside down cake!

Groundhogs, pocket-books and Easter breakfasts

:~:~:~:~:~:~:~:~:~:~:~:

"Yesterday is history. Tomorrow is a mystery. And today? Today is a gift. That's why we call it the present." ~Babatunde Olatunji

It's funny how each Spring seems as if it takes longer to get here and shorter in length. As a child, I remember what my mother termed "sweater weather" lasting much longer. But regardless of its' duration, Spring is always welcomed with open arms. Whether you are young or old, Winter takes its toll on the soul and the psyche. Long nights and cold days in Kentucky certainly can make even the most joyful of folk feel a bit depressed and wobbly inside.

I'm not sure who started the Groundhog Day charade, but that poor critter is either praised or hated every year, most of the time it's the latter. Very rarely do we exalt our furry ground-dwelling weatherman. Even though we surely realize that each year February is cold and March is only a slight improvement, we hold his shadow and his decision making skills accountable for the next 6 weeks of weather. I see quite a few of these fellas lying on the side of the road and I wonder if they were accidental deaths or intentional homicides by disgruntled drivers seeking their revenge against his ill timed shadow recognition.

I'm never surprised by cold spring starts, I can remember wearing my Easter dress under my winter coat most of my life. We have Easter pictures of my sisters and I with hats and earmuffs on our way to church with snow dusting the tulip tops in the background.

When I was smaller, my mother would get up early to prepare Easter Breakfast. She would get out the "egg cups" for our 8 minute eggs and set a table before we would even go to church. We would find our baskets the Easter Bunny hid and I would nibble off an ear of chocolate hare before Mama could stop me.

I'm not sure how my mother managed to get so much done before church, I can't even seem to get my brood up and dressed in time anymore to even get there. But she did it with aplomb and a flip of her spatula. Voila! Breakfast was served. We would eat, then rush from the table to get dressed in our McAlpin's department store finery for church.

Easter in my family meant new patent leather shoes, a new "pocket book" to match, an extremely uncomfortable dress and matching hat resting atop our ponytail. The hat was secured with a big brown bobby pin that always managed to remove part of my scalp during its insertion.

I now find myself living a life that is too comfortable sometimes. Not that I go to the grocery in my pajama pants, I'm too much of a Southern girl to leave my house without make up and a shower, but I do find myself in a t-shirt and jeans more often than not. Looking at black and white photos of my parents and their friends from years past, they all have an air of dignity and politeness as if they all just finished discussing the best recipe for Peach cobbler, all while sitting in frocked skirts, 2 inch heels and pearls.

My mother is 80 and she never leaves the house without lipstick and her belt matching her purse. I don't even wear lipstick; and the belt... it just ain't happenin'. I think the last belt I wore was the one they gave me in the maternity ward to judge my contractions. Plus any belt that would fit me would probably have to be bought by the foot from the Jethro Bodine collection at Wal-Mart, which is found in the fishing section.

Don't get me wrong, I don't want to start wearing heels and pearls to do the dishes, I'm no June Cleaver, but as a society, we have lost a certain degree of sophistication and regard for our appearance over the years. Comfort is good, but I worry that I have become too complacent in my attempt to relax. But then again, I do jobs around the house, errands and yard work that many people don't do or would prefer not to, so I suppose I do dress for the occasion. If I were to change my dress, I would most likely have to change my lifestyle, so that wouldn't work for me. Stilettos are not conducive to dog- bomb clean up.

Spring is such a relief to me, hearing the birds chirp and watching the earth come back to life every year makes my soul wake up. I may even be so inspired to make a breakfast that would rival my mothers Easter best this year, but the pearls are definitely staying in the jewelry box.

Easter Garlic Cheese Grits

Ingredients:
2 cups instant grits
3 cups boiling water
1 stick butter
8 oz extra sharp cheese (finely shredded)
1 tsp salt
1 clove garlic
2 eggs (beaten)

1. Preheat Oven to 350*

2. Stir grits into boiling water in medium sauce pan.
3. Remove from heat.
4. Stir in butter, garlic, cheese, salt and beaten eggs. Pour into well-greased or buttered glass casserole dish.
5. Bake approximately 40-50 minutes or until set and lightly browned.

This dish is best hot on its first day.

If you reheat for the next day, you may need to add water and stir after heating half way through. Leftovers can also be chilled overnight and sliced as Southern Polenta and pan fried lightly in olive oil, served alongside scrambled eggs or drizzled with Sorghum for a salty/sweet taste bud wake up!

Zen and the Art of Yard Work
:~:~:~:~:~:~:~:~:~:~:~:

Okay, I admit it, I love yard work.

What would make the common woman cringe, I delight in. Garden gloves? Who needs 'em. Dirt under my nails? Not a problem, since my ten year old has a better manicure than I do. I like the feeling of dirt in my hands. I can actually tell how my garden is going to turn out just by the color and smell of the earth it's planted in. I can't grow anything indoors, it seems that everything green that crosses our threshold is destined to lose all its leaves, turn shades of yellow and brown and then disappear. I have one houseplant that has survived a year, but I'm not sure that it will see the twinkle lights of Christmas.

There is something so basic and lovely about toiling in the dirt. The feel of the soil falling between your fingers, knowing that there is so much there I can't see that is at work. Seeing something as empty as a planted row of beans showing sprouts days later, is a miracle. The idea that a small seed can grow into something that can produce dozens of flowers or vegetables is mind boggling.

My daughter and sons love gardening with me. Sometimes when they help me "weed" the garden, it's nothing short of *deforestation*, but at least they are in there trying, and getting their hands dirty. My daughter loves the bugs in the garden. She catches them or watches them and is totally fascinated by their beauty and each of their unique jobs. She talks to the butterflies and tries to nurse ailing ladybugs back to health. Her tiny fingers reaching under rocks to pick up slugs can make even the oldest of our clan shiver with disgust. She is fearless in the yard. Nothing is unloved, or unnecessary. Everything has a purpose. She finds adoration for anything living there.

My mother in law Carolyn, loves how Lydia lights up when she talks about her bug friends, or how many beans and tomatoes she picked. Lydia is so gentle and deliberate that she can catch flies with her hands in the windowsill. Her father calls her the "fly whisperer". She can tell you most of the names of the plants in our yard and watching her beam with happiness when she has a dragonfly land on her finger is definitely a thing of beauty.

I think all children need that feeling of knowing that they are connected to the earth. That their presence here is needed not only on the earth but helping it grow and stay healthy. It wasn't until my children were older that they even understood what littering was. The idea that someone tossed a cigarette butt out of their car window, made my oldest want to call the law. He is still my litter warrior. When my wee one wanted to leave her sucker stick at the park years ago, he was quick to tell her that was wrong. I see so many adults toss out cigarette butts, wrappers and cups, even though they're right next to a garbage can. People even empty car ashtrays right onto the street at stoplights.

When I was in elementary school, we had a Conservation officer come to our class and talk to us about littering. In my school, assemblies were rare, so it was like a movie star came to visit. He was a real hero to me. I listened to every word he said, and it really made an impression on me, I wanted to "*give a hoot and not pollute*".

One of the things I remember most from my early television years, was a commercial featuring a Native American sitting bareback atop his painted pony wading through a field of litter along a polluted stream. That touched me. It truly did, I can still see that clear little tear roll down his face.

I remember years later seeing that actor on Johnny Carson, I was shocked to find out he was not a real "Indian" as I had believed, I think he was from Mexico. But his message stuck with me regardless of his deceitful ways.

I think that when you learn to appreciate the earth, and take care of it, it helps you to understand how precious life is for all of us, and how delicate the balance of life and death can be. At first, for my kids, seeing the plants die in our gardens was hard to understand. They cared for them, watered them, picked their fruit, only to see them whither and die. But that is truly what life is. We all have a life span that produces something. We all have a purpose just like the ladybug and the slug. We all have fruit to give and lessons to teach. I look at the intricate veins in a leaf and I realize that Gods work is in the leaf as well as myself. There is a force greater than nature at work in my garden.

Sometimes life in the garden is easy, when the sun is out and rain is frequent everything blooms and flourishes. Then there are times when life there is hard, when the sun is hidden by clouds and the weather turns cold, but life always goes on regardless of the hardships, something finds a way to survive.

I suppose we are a lot like plants in a garden, each of us reaching out to form friendships, marriages, families of our own, and spreading like blades of crabgrass each rooting and holding on for dear life wherever we land. I hope that the lessons learned in our garden stay with my children forever, and then hopefully they can be excellent tenders of their own.

OREO DIRT SUNDAES
(kid friendly recipe)

Vanilla, coffee or chocolate ice cream
½ package Oreos (crushed)
Gummy worms
Chocolate syrup or caramel syrup
Whipped cream topping

1. In a glass ice cream cup pack ice cream with spoon 1 inch below rim.
2. Top and drizzle with syrup of your choice.
3. Sprinkle ½ inch thick layer of Oreo "dirt" over ice cream.
4. Add cream topping (optional)
5. Add one gummy worm
6. Eat and enjoy being a kid again.

Now serving, "Service with a Smirk"
:~:~:~:~:~:~:~:~:~:~:~:~:~:~:

"A smile is a curve that sets everything straight."
~Phyllis Diller

I'm not sure how many jobs I have had. I know when I was younger, I made a list of the all the occupations and small jobs I held the first thirty years or so of my life and there were tons I had forgotten until I listed them and probably more that I can't recall, thanks to a little thing I like to call - the "1980's".

My first job in high school, I worked at the YWCA as a counselor during days for preschool and elementary kids when school was out due to snow or Holidays during the school year. That was a great introduction to learning how hard it can be to earn $3.35 cents an hour. To give you an idea of the value of a dollar then, an hour of work could buy me a Coke, fries and Big Mac in 1980, now that barely buys the burger.

At seventeen, I worked a summer at a horse farm. I loved that summer. I got extremely tan, spent most of my time outside or in a barn and the horses, they had little complaint. In fact, they were probably the best co-workers I have ever had. I grew to love the smell of sweet feed and hay, even now when I enter a barn those odors bring back fond memories.

In college I worked at Keeneland Thoroughbred Race Course for a few Spring and Fall meets. While I was attending college, I worked at least one job. I sold ladies shoes and lingerie at McAlpin's department store and did data entry for a college book factory. I worked in Medical records at a local Medical office and then after leaving college, I went on to get my barbers license, cut hair at the Marriott and one salon in Chevy Chase. Years later, I worked as a bookkeeper at Fifth Quarter steak house (where I met my wonderful husband Dave) and made automobile headlamps for General Electric Lamp plant after we were married. I think I have done a little bit of everything, so when I go out to eat dinner or shop I can appreciate the employees perspective as well as the clients. I know how hard it is to make a dollar.

However, going out for dinner take-out here in town for seafood one night, my husband and I were shocked at the public relations skills the employee at the register was lacking. She was not a youngster either. In fact, she was just dang old. I think she went to school with Mark Twain. Not that we were expecting witty conversation and fine how do you do's, but I do expect a smile for my purchase when I drop thirty-five dollars for a previously frozen take-out fried fish dinner for five with hushpuppies.

I even tried to compliment the worker on their proficiency with our order and she still didn't crack a smile. Instead she muttered a "*huh?*" followed by a well polished smirk. She looked at me like she would rather be undergoing a root canal or bikini wax instead of counting my money and engaging in polite conversation.

Of course, the first thing we thought was, if the people running the front of this restaurant are this miserable and indifferent how are the people in the back reacting to preparing our food? Are they equally as annoyed with their jobs? What quality control conditions is our food being prepared under? Should we run out the door? Yes. We should have.

I don't know about you, but I want my food prepared by caring folk, proud to do a good job and hold their work ethic in high regard. Needless to say, we won't be going back there. "Service with a smirk", does not get repeat business from the Rigneys when at all possible.

I'm not saying that all jobs need to be done with a giant fake smile, but in this economy, anyone with a job should be thankful. And anyone with a job that requires me to separate myself from my money should be thanking *me*. Times are tough for everyone. I can't imagine anyone that isn't going through some belt tightening these days. The monetary damage from a crippled economy has affected everyone's pocketbook. My savings and any *buffer* cash has been depleted and I've contemplated selling plasma for grocery money.

With all the technology we have at our fingertips, ordering pizzas on line, using the telephone and computers to pay our bills automatically and just the fact that we are staying home more, could it be that we are losing some of the social skills that make us who we are as a polite society? I see so many teenagers anymore cuss in front of my children and I when we are out in public. Where is common courtesy anymore? We have been force fed "tolerance" for so long about everything questionable that it seems like we have become an "anything goes" society. *If it feels good do it.* No matter the cost to anyone else. In our attempt to make everyone feel comfortable, we have wedged ourselves into a life of complacency and moral depletion.

I see people in their pajamas at the store, not just young people either, people my own age, people who should know better. I remember as a child, when just seeing someone in rollers was a shock. Now I see furry slippers and flannel jammies in line at the grocery. Have we no shame? Is there no limit to how self-indulged we can make ourselves? I can only imagine what is coming next. I can imagine rollaway beds with motors clanging their way to the Shop-n-Save while their passengers get a few more minutes of shut-eye.

I don't want to go out and see people in their pajamas shopping anymore than I want to see a four hundred pound gorilla fetching his milk and bread at the grocery. Seeing thirty year olds in their wash worn *"nite-nites"*, is depressing. Put on some clothes, brush your hair and teeth and wake up, your adult life is calling you.

Don't get me wrong I like flannel too. I even own blue furry slippers. I love them, they make me feel good. After a long day they make me feel relaxed. My slippers have been to the curb and back, but that's as far as they go. Raised as a southern gal, I don't even go to the mailbox without a shower and mascara.

I know some may find this simple attire trend and our lack of social and public relations skills a benign and uneventful issue. But to me it is an indicator of how our society is in decline, how our acceptance of *anything and everything* has left in its wake, nothing unacceptable.

In short, if you are working, be glad in it. The people that are coming to you and spending their money are supporting you. Without the public you would be out of a job. Be glad and thankful for that silly woman- that is probably me- that tries to talk with you at the register is so willing to part with her money to support your profession and for goodness sakes, fire the smirk and employ a smile.

Parmesan Crusted Salmon

I came up with this recipe after going to a restaurant called "Flo's place" in South Carolina one year for vacation. This has to be my all time favorite restaurant. I had never had anything like it before and for months afterwards I craved that rich creamy crusted salmon. I had to finally figure out a way to come close at home. This will do when I can't have the "real thing".

<u>Ingredients:</u>
1 full salmon filet (enough for 4 servings)
1 cup of mayonnaise (Real Mayonnaise only)
1/2 TBS dried Basil leaves (chopped fresh = 1 TBS)
1 cup Parmesan cheese

1. Preheat Oven to 375*
2. Place partially thawed Salmon filet on lightly oiled cookie sheet.
3. In a bowl mix Parmesan cheese, Mayonnaise and Basil
4. Spread mixture over top of Salmon filet, covering evenly.
5. Bake on center rack until fish is done and topping is lightly browned and bubbly.

Camping with the Princess
:~:~:~:~:~:~:~:~:~:~:~:

"*I'm Scared Mama*". I heard our 4 year old daughter's tiny voice cry out in the darkness of our pop-up camper.

I said in my most soothing voice, "*Why honey? I'm right here. Don't be scared, Mama is right here next to you.*"

Through the quiet, cricket song of night, my forty pound tiny terror replied to anyone within earshot... "*I'M SCARED I SAID!*"

Well, it was all downhill from there.

That would be the first and last summer we went camping with our daughter Lydia. We had successfully camped for years with our sons and when our daughter was born we just quit going. She was such a demanding/vocal whirling dervish, the thought of being enclosed in a small space for more than a few minutes made us all begin to itch and hyperventilate.

So with her turning 4 that July, we decided that she was ready to embark on her first camping adventure. She was in heaven when we were sitting along the banks of the Elkhorn. That day, she caught her first fish, ate her first fire roasted hot dog, had her fill in S'mores and mastered the Porta Potty. Everything was "sunshine and roses" until bedtime.

That is when the "Princess found the proverbial Pea".

Now, anyone who has been camping will probably understand that it is indeed different than home. Not only are the quarters cramped, but the beds are not exactly Sealy Posturepedics. Once the lights went out, Lydia was suddenly terrified to sleep in the pop up, even though she had played there for hours earlier.

Something happened when darkness washed over the upholstered interior and she managed to contort her tiny body into a two hundred pound cannonball. She flipped, flopped and turned. She spat, spewed and hissed. She sneezed, stretched and kicked until 3 am. Since we shared a queen size bed, I figured there was more than enough room. Wrong. Her elbows became daggers and her legs turned into jousting posts. I tried to comfort her but after a few hours, I was such a mess, I knew I had to leave with her and return home for a nights rest.

Luckily we were only a few miles from our house. So, I packed her up, and navigated past the 45 raccoons who had decided to take hwy 460 along with me in search of roadside meals. As we drove home, leaving the boys and Dad behind to enjoy the camping "experience", the Princess perked up. She sang a song and told me repeatedly how much she loved me and crooned repeated choruses of *"You are my sunshine"* until we returned to her palace. Part of me was kind of miffed that she could go from 0-60 that fast from misery to bliss. Then part of me felt empowered that I had helped with such a severe transformation. I was the Emotional Wizard. The Queen of Control, the Fixer of Fits and I rescued the rest of the family from a sleepless night by my sacrifice of the drive home.

We came inside and honestly, the house felt good. I was actually a bit relieved to be home and out of the humid July night on the creek. Having air conditioning that didn't blow on my head all night, and a mattress that was more than two inches thick was a welcomed treat. I stretched out my legs under the cool cotton sheets and secretly I was thankful that Lydia had needed to return home. I felt guilty that I had to leave the males in our clan back at the pop up, but so thankful for our beds and comfort and in no time, I was dreaming of soft pillows and paradise in my King-size for one.

We slept in, snuggled for a bit in the morning before we returned to the campground and found that the boys had been up for hours, thanks to the early morning sun, and they had decided to go for a swim. Breakfast had been eaten and they had all slept *fairly* well after I took the "town crier" home. We stayed and feasted all day on snacks, and caught so many fish that we went through an entire container of red worms.

That evening, we had steak on the fire and another round of flaming marshmallows. It was a perfect day. When it was bedtime I didn't even try to force Lydia to sleep in the camper, I told my sons and husband I would be taking her back home and if anyone wanted to go with me they could. I assumed they would all balk at the idea. After all, they were "Real men". Communicating without words, their decision was made and my SUV seats were full on the way back to the house.

Within 50 minutes every Rigney was in their cool cotton sheets stretched out and sound asleep. While it had initially been the Princess finding the Pea, it turned into the entire Royal Family finding their own pods.

It's been years since that trip along the Elkhorn and my daughter wants to go camping again. I have to admit that I miss those lazy days by the creek and the thrill of packing up fishing gear, Twinkies and pan-fried chicken. I miss a crackling hot campfire at night and the coolness of light dew that forms on the picnic table and cooler in the morning. How the world wakes up earlier in a campground, how the camaraderie exists there from site to site and how it makes a memory just because of the smells, tastes and sounds that exist only when camping.

However, when we do decide to venture out into the woods or on the creek again, I may take an extra air mattress for the Princess, just to make sure bedtime is drama-free.

One Skillet Camp Supper

When we go camping, we take very little in regards to cookware. It weighs too much. So anytime we can do a one-skillet meal, it makes it easier. This is savory, easy and don't be surprised if everyone asks for seconds.

Ingredients:
1 lb. bulk mild breakfast sausage
1 chopped green bell pepper
1 chopped medium white onion (Vidalia is best)
1 small can of evaporated milk
1 can cream of mushroom soup
1 package of light and fluffy noodles

1. In large sauce pan, cook noodles according to package directions.
2. Drain. Set aside in serving bowl and return large sauce pan to stove.
3. Cook Sausage in saucepan with pepper and onion.
~ Crumble and break up sausage as it cooks. When sausage mixture is no longer pink, drain fat. Return pepper/onion/sausage mix to pan. Add mushroom soup and evaporated milk. Stir in noodles, cook until bubbling and serve with bread or biscuits.

A fumbling, tumbling, food Addict's confession

:~:~:~:~:~:~:~:~:~:

I eat my feelings. I know I do. Sometimes after a hard day I will catch myself physically "stuffing" my face with food. More than once, I've answered the phone and tried to say *"Hello"* and not even realized I had my mouth to maximum capacity +4 until crumbs went flying into my cleavage.

Whenever possible, I exercise, I go to the gym and I try so very hard to shave these hips and he-man thighs down to a respectable size, but they just love me. They won't leave.

I never imagined I would be this large woman that I am. But even though I was average size in high school, probably considered thin by today's standards, because I was tall- I just always thought of myself as the "big girl". I think I just became my own self fulfilled prophecy.

I try to keep my carbohydrates to a minimum, I don't consume many processed sugars or high calorie foods, but I will even take eating lettuce to a new level...and eat nearly an entire head in one or two days, all by myself. I like to eat. Plain and simple, it calms me.

I grew up thin. Long and thin. "Gangly" is what my mother called me. She said I grew too fast, that's why my legs ached so much in the middle of the night. I stumbled, fell down steps, ran into walls and spent half of my fifth grade summer sleeping in a Lazy-boy because I fell down the second floor steps and broke my ribs.

My "tween" years were like living in a remote controlled body; A body that was operated from the next room by a blind man with missing thumbs.

Awkward- didn't even begin to describe my constant collisions with stationary objects. I spilled my milk almost every meal, to the point that my sisters avoided sitting where the crack in the center of the wooden dinner table was, because it would consistently head in that direction and leak cold white moo-juice onto their knees.

Still, every night my mother gave me a glass of milk. Each dinner she would say, *"Now watch this glass, be careful"* and most of the time I managed it, but inevitably just as we would accept spillage as a thing of my past, I would reach and tumble the amber glass onto the table and scatter sisters. But over time, I mastered the glass and they returned to the great divide with dry knees.

My mother was either extremely patient of very forgetful.

I'm not sure why I find so much comfort with food. Perhaps it's the memories of the times shared at the table with my family. Maybe it's reminiscent of the aromas my mother flavored our nostrils with thanks to her fine country cooking. But I have had a love affair with food for what seems most of my adult life.

My husband loves me like I am. My kids always referred to my lap as *"comfy...like a pillow"* and they seem to think there is no greater place on earth than feeling a wrap in my flabby flying-squirrel arms when they've had a bad day, but I really need to get myself in order and figure out exactly what makes me feel so good about feeling so full.

But everyone has a cross to bear I suppose. I just wish mine was edible, then my problem would be solved and it would be, delicious.

"I arta Choke You" Dip

For some reason, every time we mention artichokes in my family we call 'em *"I arta choke you's"* Not sure why, I'm sure it started a long time ago when one my uncles or aunts came up with it, but regardless, this dip is sublime. High in calories and fat but low in effort and produces a great *appeteaser* for parties or friends that drop by. There will be no leftovers.

Ingredients:
1 can or jar of artichoke hearts
1 cup of REAL mayonnaise
1 cup of parmesan cheese
1 box of Wheat Thins or Triscuits

1. Drain artichoke hearts and then chop.
2. Mix all ingredients together and pour into a 8 or 9 inch round baking dish.
3. Bake at 350* for 20-25 minutes until browned and bubbly. Serve with Triscuits, Wheat Thins or a healthy cracker that can handle the weight!

The Winter of Our Contentment
:~:~:~:~:~:~:~:~:~:~:~:

"When I no longer thrill to the first snow of the season, I'll know I'm growing old." ~Lady Bird Johnson

I'm over forty and I still love that first snow fall and that first snow day and actually any ones that follow. Being able to turn off the alarm for school and go back to sleep is my idea of the perfect start to a wintry morning. For some reason the sheets and the bed seem more appealing after the alarm clock rings.

Now, I'm not crazy, I'm not cut out for home schoolin', so sometimes, that "perfect" start to my morning wears thin around lunchtime with three kids confined to the house and arguments over the remote control ensue.

Unfortunately for some parents, the announcement of school closing brings on the agony and the stress of trying to find a babysitter for the day at 6am, or the concern of leaving their teens home all day unsupervised with the pantry and fridge at their disposal, but I can't help it, I'm spoiled rotten. I love a snow day.

In my town, even with a snow plan, a few inches of snow or a thin layer of ice makes some roads impassable by four-wheel drive, much less a huge, yellow school bus. When I see those words about school closings roll across the bottom of the television through my early morning crusted eyes, it brings back fond memories of the Winter of 1978. I was a 9th grader in Fayette County at the time and it was almost unheard of for school to be cancelled. We went Hell or high water.

So, when we had a snow day, you could bet it meant that the county was literally crippled. There was something very exciting about the idea that no one could leave their home by car. My pioneering spirit came out and I made it my mission to recruit kids for constructing snow forts and building Goliath snowmen who looked remarkably like everybody's Daddy since they'd all be wearing their hats and scarves. I interrupted many a quiet Cap'n Crunch morning with a rap at my neighbor's doors begging them to come out and play before the sun had settled in the cloudy sky.

Most of us did not own snow boots, so we saved our "Rainbo" and "Wonder" bread bags and slipped them on between two layers of tube socks. Believe it or not, this worked great. It was a struggle to get double socks into your leather Adidas, but we managed.

We would be outside for hours. Literally. Noses dripping, herds of red cheeked Yeti's having the time of our lives. We would go inside at lunch to thaw, wipe our numb noses on something other than our sleeves and return to the bright white snow covered suburbs with full bellies of warm Campbell's tomato soup and toasty grilled cheese. That winter of '78 was so fierce that later, in the spring, you could find *"I survived the winter of '78"* t-shirts for sale at the local K-Mart.

Our school superintendent at that time drove my mother and every mother in the county crazy when it came to snow days. Even if it had snowed eight inches overnight, he would never announce school closing until nearly time to leave for the bus. Many mornings I would be putting on my coat, waiting at the radio for the news. He was not the most popular man and it seemed like he lived forever.

Because of the unbelievable winter of '78, we missed nearly an entire month of school due to the snow and ice. When we finally did return, the cleared parking lot had a pile of snow that touched the roof of my junior high school. It was so monstrous that it didn't completely disappear until late May.

Spring break was surrendered that year, but most of us were okay with that. We'd vacationed at home the entire month of February. We also had to go one extra hour after school for weeks and attended school on a few Saturday. This was weird. I don't think we got much done, even the teachers seemed confused. But it was all worth it, the memories of my bread bag socks and mile high forts is something I will remember much longer than any school work I had to make up.

That freak winter storm of snow and ice may be just a page for the record books, but for me and my frozen friends of '78 we will never forget it and for my mother, she won't either.

She and I spent many hours together during those days when it was too cold and icy outside to play. We played rounds of Go-Fish, watched The Price is Right and Match Game, squeezed in a soap opera or two, munched on Charle's Chips and drank hot chocolate well into the afternoons. She told me stories of her own snow covered childhood. By 4 o'clock I would help her get dinner ready for my father who braved the ice everyday to get to the factory where he worked. Each night I would pray for snow to fall as high as the windows and a chance to live it all again the next day.

I wouldn't be surprised if my kids ask for the same thing when winter arrives and I wouldn't be surprised if their prayers aren't answered a few times too.

Or at least I hope so.

Pizza in a cup

We love chili. Any kind of chili. This chili seems to be a favorite of everyone. We even came in 2nd place in a chili cook-off with this recipe. We just call it "Pizza in a cup." Warms you on a Winters day and still can be a great addition to the Super Bowl party or maybe a great meal for Game- night gathered around the kitchen table for a few rounds of Rook with friends.

Ingredients:
2 cans of Italian style stewed tomatoes
2 pounds of ground beef
2 cans kidney beans (rinsed and drained)
1 jar of pizza sauce
12 oz. tomato paste
1 ½ cups of tomato juice
1 12 oz can tomato sauce
6 oz of sliced pepperoni
1 cup chopped green pepper
1 chopped onion
1 tsp Italian seasoning
1 tsp hot pepper flakes (Optional)

1. Cook beef until no longer pink. Drain.
2. In large stock pot, add all ingredients including drained beef.
3. Bring to a boil. Reduce heat. Simmer 45 minutes.
4. Garnish with shredded mozzarella cheese and serve with garlic toast.

Green apple shampoo and a spiritual Cleansing
:~:~:~:~:~:~:~:~:~:~:~:~:

"Any fool can count the seeds in an apple. Only God can count all the apples in one seed". ~Robert H. Schuller

I was in seventh grade when I had my first Christian camp experience. I went with my best friend Carol; she was one year older than me. We went to her First Assembly church sponsored camp about two hours from our homes. I can't even remember the name of the town it was in, I just know it was a long drive in her mother's '69 sky blue VW wagon to get there and each mile separated from my Mama seemed like an eternity as I had never been that far from home before.

Carol and I were the type of girls that would play for hours outside hitting a badminton birdie back and forth across the net in her back yard trying to break our old record of continuous hits. We loved breaking our own records...Longest time throwing a ball back and forth, longest time tossing a Frisbee, most consecutive somersaults...We grew up making mud pies, playing kick ball and riding bikes. We were innocents. We were outdoors from early morning until time to turn out the porch light.

So when we went to camp, being exposed to girlie girls that were accustomed to being away from home was a new experience for us. The first day we were sent to the "girl's showers" we stared in silent shock at all the naked girls taking showers without shower curtains and without speaking a word, gathered our towels and returned to our cabin with a collective determination never to enter those doors again. The idea of showering in front of someone else was too much for us, not to mention the spiders we immediately spotted in the corners of the room and nesting in the high ceiling corners.

So, we decided to turn our little half bath we shared into our own bathing station. We washed our hair in the sink with our "Agree Green Apple" shampoo and even though we probably stunk to high heaven, our hair was clean and we hoped our "Tickle!" deodorant would mask our scent. In our minds we were doing the right thing, who could expect us to shower under such freakish conditions? Surely our mothers would understand why we had to go without a proper bath for a week.

Being raised in a Southern Baptist church, we were pretty formal in our service. The preacher preached, we listened, sang a few verses of "Shall we gather at the river" and someone would decide to follow Jesus and end up baptized a week later. We would finish up service with *"Praise God from whom all blessings flow"*, shake hands and do it all again 7 days later. When I got to camp and saw how different their approach to praising God was I felt a bit out of place.

I was used to a very structured Sunday with the focus of the sermon being aimed primarily at subjects I had difficulty understanding. While at camp, there were more kids than I had ever seen gathered to praise. Approximately 200 of us sat on hay bales under the shelter staring at a stage with the youngest evangelists I had ever run across. There were songs, tambourines, harmonicas, guitars and a jubilance I had never seen in the walls of my own church. Although it was awkward, for the first time in my life, I felt a connection I never had before. What a monumental experience that was for me.

It was almost as though all the things I had learned in my church had been called into action and I finally understood the power of God and how he could affect my life by celebrating him with complete strangers. As if my soul had decided to wake up and take notice that the world was indeed aware of a power greater than ours, that Gods word wasn't just something I shared on Sundays with my family and other members of our church. It finally all made sense to me. But it took getting out of my routine in order for it to surface.

By the time our week was up, Carol and I had matured greatly. I left my house a girl and came back a much wiser version of myself, oh and by not bathing for a week, a much more "odiferous" version of myself. Oddly enough, I never went back to church camp. It may have something to do with the look on my mothers face when she opened my duffel bag full of dirty clothes or the odor I presented her with when I gave her my welcome home hug...but I think I didn't return because I knew my experience would never be as true and pure as that Summer.

But that wonderful week of soul cleansing, green apple shampoo and my first steps at spiritual independence will always be a sweet and meaningful part of who I am.

Sleep over Camp Sloppy Joes

Prepare yourself, once you make these, canned mixes will never do. Your family will request these at least 2 times a month. They are easy and make a great hot dog chili with leftovers.

Ingredients:
1 and ½ pounds of ground beef
6 oz of ketchup
4 oz of water
1 TBS vinegar
3 TBS brown sugar
1 heaping tsp mustard
2 tsp A-1 steak sauce
2 tsp Worcestershire sauce
1 TBS BBQ sauce
1 small diced onion
2 dashes of Tabasco sauce

Cook beef and onion in skillet until no longer pink, drain grease. Return to skillet and add remaining ingredients. Stir and simmer on low for 1 hour. Stir occasionally. Serve on soft buns. (Makes approximately 8 Sloppy Joes)

Chicken soup for the Neighborhood
:~:~:~:~:~:~:~:~:~:~:~:~:~:~:

"Soup is a lot like a family. Each ingredient enhances the others; each batch has its own characteristics"
~Marge Kennedy

When I was about 12, my mother decided she was going to make homemade chicken noodle soup. This task didn't seem like anything she couldn't handle, since she was known in the neighborhood as the wife of a "hunter". She had cooked up everything from squirrel and grouse to buffalo and elk. She was the queen of the pressure cooker and the master of the marinade. So, she truly had made just about everything else, except for some reason chicken soup expertise had evaded her grasp.

When I left for school that morning, she was getting ready to start her cooking and she seemed very optimistic. Since I love eating, thoughts about her soup were with me all day. While at school, I imagined a steaming pot of soup waiting for me after I got off the bus. I have always found a certain romance or love for cooking and eating. For me, many lessons have been learned in the kitchen with my mother. It seems like the kitchen truly is the heart of the home.

My mother originally started out that morning with one lonesome chicken, then believed that it wasn't enough and added another whole de-feathered friend to the stock. She cut, diced and prepared vegetables for her soup, and then once the chicken had stewed, she realized that she had too much stock and chicken and not enough vegetables, so she cut up more vegetables.

Bring on a bigger pot.

Before she knew it she was adding more of everything until she had vats of chicken soup on every burner in the kitchen and reserves in pots on the counters.

Her venture into soup for one family turned into soup for the entire

South end of the county before she knew it. When I imagine her there alone with her out of control soup factory, all I see is an "I Love Lucy" episode unfolding, minus one frantic Ethel. We laugh about her "endless soup" now, but I can remember how disheveled she looked having chicken soup coming out of her ears when I got home. There were so many pots, large and small sitting around the kitchen, it looked as though our roof was leaking broth.

I have my share of overdoing and underestimating tasks myself. I had a solo furniture shopping expedition when David and I first got married that went terribly awry. Out of the blue, I went out and bought a two thousand dollar, ginormous three piece sectional sofa that would not even fit through our apartment door. We had to carry it over the back deck and through the sliding doors. It took up our entire living room. It had two recliners, a full size bed and a corner piece that seated three more.

That couch nearly broke us in more ways than one. I had put it on a furniture store credit card and it took so many years to pay it off that we laughingly refer to it now as our "ten thousand dollar couch". But I can tell you, David didn't find anything funny about it over 20 years ago. It took a while for him to stop saying, "*Don't bring home a two thousand dollar couch*" every time I went out the door with my purse.

Thank goodness we both forgave me for trying to live like a Rockefeller. Over time it seems like those things that were so big and troublesome have deflated. Time changes so much, it can mend hearts, change perspectives and make memories fonder, even if at first it seems like a nightmare.

When our first son William arrived, I thought I had totally prepared myself for parenting. I had read all the magazines I could, babysat for my sisters for what seemed like my entire life, and still I was unprepared.

Looking back at those early years of new parenting, what seemed like impossible days and near nervous breakdowns are actually comforting and sweet. That old house we lived in with drafts and cold walls just made us sit closer together and snuggle a bit tighter. I remember when it was time to give William a bath on the kitchen counter when he was just an infant, we would turn on the oven and open its door just to warm up the room it was so chilly in that tiny kitchen.

In the winter we actually had ice form on the "inside" of the single pane windows. It seemed like it was one repair after another in our first little fixer-upper, every bit of extra money went into that house. When one thing got fixed, something else would break. I thought I would be glad to be rid of that place. But when we pass through our old neighborhood, we'll sometimes take a minute to drive by. When we do, it's as if we are seeing an old friend that we miss. David and I grow silent and let the moment wash over us and we are so grateful for our eight years there, we learned so much in that little house, it was time well spent, regardless of the cost.

When I think about my Moms soup incident, it reminds me how quickly things we think we can manage can get out of control, and before we know it we are up to our ears in excess troubles and soupy mess. Mama may have only been making soup but her cooking lesson went well beyond the kitchen. But that could just be the writer in me trying to see beyond the obvious.

Now, with all this talk about Mamas and homemade chicken soup, maybe it's time for me to try and make some myself. Who knows what I may end up with; I just hope I have enough pots and enough patience.

Easy One Pot Chicken Noodle Soup

Ingredients:
4-6 chicken breasts (skinless/boneless)
6 12 oz. cans chicken broth
8 stalks celery (diced)
8 carrots (diced)
1 bag of egg noodles or No Yolks Noodles

In a crock pot, place 4 raw chicken breasts (boneless/skinless) in the bottom.
Pour 6 cans broth over raw chicken.
Toss in diced carrots.
Top with diced celery.
Turn crock pot on HI.
DO NOT stir.

Cook 5 hours. Remove and shred the cooked chicken.
Return to broth, stir in 1 package of noodles and continue to cook on HI for 35 minutes.
Add salt and pepper as desired.
Serve!
Tastes great the next day!

From Pizza man to Rocket Science
:~:~:~:~:~:~:~:~:~:~:~:~:~:

"Adults are always asking little kids what they want to be when they grow up because they're looking for ideas." ~Paula Poundstone

One lazy afternoon when my daughter Lydia was about four years old, she looked at me in the rear view mirror of our car and let out a long sigh as she watched cows pass by behind the long winding black fences on our way home... *"Mama, I'm not sure what I'm gonna be when I grow up...I'm thinkin' astronaut, artist or space alium...."*

When she finished her declaration, a certain look of satisfaction spread across her face as if she had just narrowed down all the decisions for the next twenty years and now all she had to do was sit back and enjoy the ride. At that very moment, I saw myself in her reflection, a part of me that existed years ago and had dreams of my own of conquering the world. I found her satisfactory smile also wash across my own face at the simplicity of her resolve and her adoration for all things possible.

As my oldest son, talks about college majors that seem interesting and exciting but ultimately offer very little either in pay or job marketability, I have a hard time keeping the reality of such a poor career choice to myself without looking like the "Career Czar" and dashing his dreams of days filled with exploration and discovery. For some reason I feel compelled to tether his high hopes to my *rock-of-reason* and I really need to stop, but it's difficult. I have to remember that his ideas and zeal at thinking outside of the box are what allow us to reach for the stars and not keep our feet cemented in mediocrity and self loathing.

From the time our children are born, we speculate about what type of adults they will become. We encourage good grades and reward them when they succeed, we fill their heads with college or trade school thoughts and point them in a direction that we hope will ultimately provide them with a way to earn enough money to support themselves and finally move out of the nest taking our old couches, used refrigerators and outdated kitchen tables in the process.

No parent worth their weight in salt doesn't have times where they silently wish for a quieter house and clear view of the driveway where they can watch their independently wealthy kids pull up for a Sunday meal. Only to leave hours later for their own homes leaving us with a few dirty dishes and happy memories of a well spent Sunday. But I have learned over the years that wealth comes in many forms other than monetary. It also comes as health, happiness and finding the right person to share your life with. We ultimately want our children living up to all that they can be and living a blessed life where they feel worthy and necessary.

Sitting here now, with an apron pocket full of lost Leg-os, Barbie shoes, stray barrettes and rogue crayons, I can't imagine that the day will arrive when our three *mini-me's* will leave the nest. They seem so young and helpless in this great big world. I can't imagine that they will ever be able to clean their own dishes without being told or sort their laundry without making their entire wardrobe gray or pink. But I know that day will be here sooner than I would like and there will be tears flowing when that old furniture is loaded in the bed of a truck making its exit from our house to begin a new life.

When all is said and done, as parents, all we really want for our kids is for them to be happy. We don't really know exactly what they will become when they grow up, even though we've heard every career from "Pizza Delivery man" to "rocket scientist" mentioned before they even reach first grade. With each milestone they pass as toddlers we delve into their little psyches in hopes of capturing a glimpse of what their hidden talents will be by prompting them with everything from toy fire trucks to washable crayons.

In the end, life is unpredictable and career choices don't always add up to life choices. I've seen people with college majors working as department store clerks, and people with very little education going far in the workplace with only determination and a will to succeed on their resume'. So for me my only wish for my children when they graduate is that they find peace and a life worthy of living to the fullest, whether it's in a fire truck or a space suit.

"When Life Give's you Lemons" Lemonade Pie

It's true, sometimes life does give you lemons, but I prefer Lemonade pie to just plain ol' lemonade. Try this when you've got time to wait overnight for a dessert. Great for Summer cookouts by the pool or the creek.

Ingredients:
1 14oz. can of sweetened condensed milk
1 TBS lemon juice or juice of 1 lemon
1 16 oz tub of non-dairy whipped topping
6 oz frozen lemonade concentrate
1 graham cracker crust shell

1. Combine all ingredients.
2. Pour into graham cracker pie shell.
3. Freeze overnight.
4. Set out 15 minutes prior to slicing.

Did I miss my own Mid-Life Crisis?
:~:~:~:~:~:~:~:~:~:~:~:~:~:~:~:

"Mom, have you had your mid-life crisis yet?" My teenage son William asked, while eating a handful of Pringles leaning in the doorway to my room. Oblivious to the fact he had now opened a Pandora's Box of emotions for me to consider. Instead, he was acting as though he had just asked if the mail had run.

I smiled, and jokingly told him I didn't think so, but I had been pretty busy with the laundry and for all I knew it could be happening right now.

Then he asked, *"Well, how about Dad, has he had his yet?"*

I assured him that neither of us was entering any life altering stages, and then I went back to folding the clothes, which I suddenly noticed had become my life's work. I was pretty sure David hadn't shown any signs of a mid-life change yet. Surely, I would have noticed. I had always heard a mid life crisis was more noticeable with men than women. Of course, I heard this from other women. I hate to stereotype, but don't most men buy a fancier car, a bigger boat or more hair during their midlife crisis?

But then I felt a slight pang of fear, I mentioned the other day how much I would like a boat, and my car is getting older...

I found a way to pacify my fear with the fact that I am only forty-seven. Then, of course, I did the math, multiplying my age by two, only to find a double digit blinking *white hot* in my brain. Hmmmm, maybe I am due for this "crisis" soon. Then, I had a worry that I had already gone through it, without really knowing, since I feel in "crises" a lot of the time. Maybe I had it when the dryer went out? Or maybe when I was going through my detox of depression medication? Then I remembered all the ranting and raving done around here on a regular basis anymore that I used to blame on PMS or hormones before my hysterectomy and I started to panic.

It even occurred to me that I was experiencing my midlife crisis now and that all this self-inventory and evaluation was just a part of the process. Surely not, I am too busy for a life change of that magnitude. I have things to do and people that depend on me to be in top notch "Mother Mode" twenty four hours a day seven days a week. Just missing a dose or two of my thyroid medication sends me off track. I can't go freaking out or falling apart right now, I just got myself back together for Pete's sake!

Oh my goodness, did I just say "*Pete's sake?*" I am old.

I do recall my biological clock going off a few years ago, and now it doesn't even tick anymore. I used to see a newborn baby and long for another one, now I see those sweet toes and tiny hands and feel relief that mine are out of diapers and I can finally sleep through the night and step out of the house without a babysitter.

I do love babies, but I am too old to lose anymore sleep and too tired to fight the fight. Oh my gosh, I am nearly old enough to be a Grammaw! Thank goodness I waited to have kids, so I am at least 7 or 8 years away from being a Grandparent. Even though my mind is already arriving and preparing a place for me.

So, I guess I should get this ball rolling for my mid-life adventure. What should I do first? Change my hair? It's already shorter than my sons and I would look awful as a blonde. I considered Lap band surgery, but that was too much of a commitment for me, the idea of floating plastic parts inside my body was too much. I don't like getting procedures done anyway; I had mercury fillings in my teeth for 35 years for Pete's Sake. Oh my, there I go again using poor *Peter*. I have to find a new saying.

I know- Maybe I will talk with David and see if we can plan our mid-life journey together. Maybe we could plan on having this wacky trip to our fifties at the same time, who knows, maybe we could both get new cars, but there is no way I am letting David become a member of the Hair Club for Men.

Actually, I just can't imagine surrendering to any type of turn in life that changes who I am. I know that it's taken me years to come to terms with the fact that I can not be the perfect mother or the perfect wife. Regardless of how hard I try, my kids are eventually going to look back and find fault with my parenting, and pick some obscure off-day I had to tell me that I somehow scarred them for life. No matter how much I would like to imagine that I am Carol Brady, I still send my husband off to work with wrinkled pants, I burn biscuits on a regular basis and I don't always know where my purse is. But I have attained a certain peace about being imperfect and the fact that I am just an average mother and wife doing the best she can is a comfortable fit for me.

So actually, maybe I have had my crisis, I just didn't think of it as a bad thing, more of a mid-life "realization". I have managed to find out that life is too short to dwell on things we can't change, or sweat the stuff that really isn't as important as the world would have us believe.

Besides, I don't have to worry about menopause now that I've been *spayed*...but I will have to change my patch prescription now and then...

...by the way, is it hot in here or is it just me?

Peter-Peter pumpkin Bread

Pumpkin is so underrated. Its use is primarily limited to Fall dishes but it is available year 'round in a can. Use it more often and you will fall in love with its versatility to add moisture in cakes, cookies and create the perfect bread.

Ingredients:
1 cup canned pumpkin
1/3 cup of water
½ cup of vegetable oil
2 eggs
1 and 2/3 cup of flour
1 and ¼ cup of sugar
1 tsp of baking soda
½ tsp of cinnamon
½ tsp nutmeg
½ tsp salt

Mix pumpkin, water, vegetable oil and eggs. In same bowl, add all the dry ingredients, stir and mix well. Pour into floured and greased loaf pan. Bake at 350* for 55-60 minutes.

"I be Betty"
:~:~:~:~:~:~:~:~:~:~:

*"Love all, trust a few, do wrong to none". ~*William Shakespeare

Is it just me or is every phone call I receive anymore regarding bills and charities from a thick-accented Indian woman named "Betty"? She speaks through choppy and often indistinguishable pronunciations of the English language and tries very hard to get her hands on my bank account.

Between her accent and mine, it's a struggle to communicate. I have trouble following the hurried confabs of my Northern neighbors, much less engaging with a West Indies fast-talker.

It seems no matter who I call for customer service, I get *Miss Betty*. She must work a lot of overtime, and for some reason she just can't take "*No*" for an answer. About midway through her 30 minute rant about why I need her services she tries many attempts to persuade me to see things her way. Betty tries to set me at ease by making comments about how the weather is "*troubling*" or how beautiful "*Kaintookee*" is this time of year as if to con me into believing she is just downtown at her desk watching the Scott County morning farm traffic pass by her office window. I can't help but envision a different version; where Betty sits poised in her cubicle, me on speaker phone, halfway across the world with her boss standing by her side prompting her methodic approach towards gaining the release of my financial records.

Even when I tell her I am busy or can't talk she seems to interpret my words as a request to continue her lengthy suggestion list on how to pay my bill or how eager she is to have me volunteer my savings to support her cause or charity that I most often have never heard of. Many times she wakes me on a sleepy Saturday before the crickets have even stopped singing their night song outside my window. This pre-dawn approach will not end well.

During my confabs with dear ol' Betty, she asks me repeatedly to give her my financial and bank account information, even though each time I decline to do so. She reassures me that it is confidential and secure, but honestly I find it hard to believe a woman speaking to me from another Country in the middle of what is obviously their time to sleep. Betty just doesn't make my list of people that I want to trust with that information and honestly, waking me up before my kids on a Saturday morning to remind me my new dishwasher payment is due, is enough to put you on my naughty list.

Perhaps my favorite thing that Betty does is when she tries to convince me that I don't know who I am. She will call with a wrong number and then ask me to verify my own identity by giving her "just the last 4 digits of my social security number". As if I had walked around for years not knowing my real name and lived under the guise of someone else because of a near-death experience causing me to live in a prolonged state of Amnesia; waiting for that one phone call where those four magic numbers would be uttered in heavy accent via phone and I would awake from my catatonic slumber only to reclaim my debts and pay them gladly for giving me rise from my long dark night of ignorance.

Betty is a hoot.

I'm not sure why nearly the entire country is outsourced. We have so many people eager to work here, why employ the rest of the world first? I realize it's cost efficient, probably saves the companies millions by hiring outside the U.S. But I would think that those jobs they create by staying here are going to help pay those bills and fund the charities they keep calling everyone about.

But what do I know? I'm just an Amnesiac from Kaintookee.

"Fuhgettaboutit" Slow Cooker Lasagna

Not the typical layered dish, this is a way to get the flavor of a hearty Lasagna without all the fuss and clean up. Just a few steps from start to finish but the aroma of Sicily will fill the halls and bring hungry tummies waiting at the kitchen table.

1 lb. Ground beef
1 lb. bulk sausage (Italian or breakfast is fine)
2 jars marinara sauce
2 cup sliced mushrooms
12 large cans Italian Tomatoes (not drained)
9 – 12 oz bag frozen cheese stuffed ravioli or tortellini (set out to thaw in fridge overnight)
Shredded Mozzarella

Brown the meats. Drain. Place the browned meat and all ingredients except for pasta in your crock pot. Cook on LOW for 5-6 hours. Turn up to HI, add dry Pasta last 40 minutes. Just drop it right in and cover tightly.

Top with shredded Mozzarella and serve with garlic bread.
Usually no leftovers! Serves 6-8.

When I get to Heaven, can I ask God for ice cream?
:~:~:~:~:~:~:~:~:~:~:~:~:~:

While riding her bike in the driveway, our daughter Lydia, who was six years old at the time, hopped off to give me a kiss. Out of the blue, she said that she was glad about us going to heaven someday, and I told her I was happy about it too. Then she asked, *"Mama, when I get to heaven can I ask God for ice cream?"*

I thought about it only for second and then I said, *"Sure you can."* I realized that having ice cream at your disposal was probably a six year olds idea of heaven. She smiled and went back to riding up and down the driveway with a look of true satisfaction on her face.

It's easy to forget how simple a child's desires are. With all the fit throwing that sometimes erupts around here, it seemed unusual that an idea so simple and sweet could tame the wild beast in our smallest, yet loudest Rigney.

It reminded me of when I was young and we would make homemade ice cream. It was usually on vacation or at a family reunion. So much work was involved I now understand why we did it so rarely. But at the time, I wanted to do it every Sunday. It never failed that some Miller much-too-small would volunteer to "churn" and before long their little arms would wear out. Daddy would be left cranking intermittently until the big wooden bucket would finally yield its sweet, heavenly confection, in flavors of banana or strawberry. No other ice cream tastes like homemade banana ice cream. It's a glorious delight all to itself, and I don't even like bananas that much.

Speaking of reunions, isn't it funny how most of the old photos surrounding any reunions or family get-togethers seem like they were held during some awful heat wave? Everyone has a paper hand fan and you can almost bet there is going to be someone sacked out under the shade of a fruit tree. It could be because everyone seems to have on so much clothing. Most of the men in the photos have on button down shirts and slacks and almost every head is covered with a dark hat. But let's not forget the ladies, not only are most of them in dresses, they have hairdo's that look as though they took entire cans of Aqua Net hairspray and *Dippity-Do* to hold their giant cylindrical shapes.

My mother was a big fan of the "beehive up-do". When we went to Sanibel Island, Florida when I was nine, she kept her hair up the entire time. She managed to keep her coif safe from the salty air, the pool and the deployed cargo of flying seagulls. Safely tucked away inside her purple head scarf and bobby-pinned side curls, her hairdo survived a vacation that required two days of driving in a car with three girls and no air conditioning.

I'm not worthy by comparison. By the end of the day, not only does my hair look tired, but my make up has usually gone "south" and landed somewhere near my chin. So my Mama, she's my hero.

When my daughter asked me about ice cream and heaven, it really wasn't necessary to go into the details of whether we would need to eat in heaven or searching for biblical verses to quote. Because I think that we all have our own ideas of heaven. We can read the passages of the bible to understand what awaits us, but for all of us, I suppose there is a hope that heaven holds for us all the things that make our lives here on earth lovely and bring us happiness.

When I imagine what heaven is like, I always imagine gardens and flowers of endless color that smell of Sweet Pea and herbs. A garden so fragrant with flowers that I am overcome with joy, just from the aroma of their creation; surrounded by my family in an endless afternoon of bliss and comfort.

Now that I think about it, those afternoons where we churned our own ice cream, under the shade of an old apple tree were pretty close to heaven. Maybe I can introduce my kids to a bit of heaven on earth and bring out that old ice cream churn in the attic that was handed down to me few years ago from my father.

I am sure my youngest will volunteer first then tucker out. But she has two older brothers that will take it over until the end, and if not, I am sure their Daddy will finish the work for them. After all, he's a fan of ice cream too.

Heavenly Ice Cream Salad

This just may be the easiest recipe ever. Nobody can resist this cool, smooth and refreshing dessert. Great to take to someone that may be recovering from a cold, just feeling a bit under the weather or as the finishing touch to an outdoor barbecue.

Ingredients:
2 small boxes of lemon gelatin mix
2 cups hot water
8oz cream cheese
1 quart of vanilla ice cream
1 small can of crushed pineapple (in juice)

Combine all ingredients. Stir until blended well and then chill in the refrigerator for 4 hours or until set. Overnight works best. Enjoy!!!

Memories in Brown Corduroy
:~:~:~:~:~:~:~:~:~:~:~:

"I love my father as the stars - he's a bright shining example and a happy twinkling in my heart." ~Terri Guillemets

I suppose there is nothing as precious as the relationship between a parent and child. Few things hold their influence over a lifetime like that of a Father. Fortunately, I was blessed with a wonderful one and his love for me and lessons that he taught have served me well.

In fact, it was who he was as a man that made me marry such a fine one. My Father taught me early on in life that I was someone that mattered. I wasn't left at home when he had errands, he took me with him and I knew the local butcher by name as well as his barber. I sat many mornings watching him bowl at the local lanes with his G.E. teammates, quietly sipping a cherry coke. Being with him was the safest place in the world. I remember kids at school saying things to one another like, "*My Dad can beat up your Dad*", and I smiled inside knowing that they obviously hadn't seen my Daddy, because he was the Goliath of Fathers. My gentle giant.

At church on Sundays when the sermon no longer held my interest, I would reach over and hold my fathers hand. I would be amazed at his colossal thumb and the huge half moon on his nail. Turning his hand over onto mine to measure it, my hand would disappear under his. He had a few calluses and cuts, an oil stain or two in the prints of his fingertips, but they were beautiful to me.

My Father never hit me with those hands. That is not necessarily saying that I didn't deserve it at times. But it was the "look" that was given by my Father that kept his three girls in line. He didn't have to say much; just a look of disappointment or a stern glance usually did the trick. We all wanted the approval of our Father, because we mattered to him.

I'm learning as I get older, that regardless of age, you are always considered a child in the eyes of your parents. At least that's how it is with mine. This can be a blessing and a curse.

While the rest of the world is aging and becoming wiser, my sisters and I are caught in a web of being "forever young" according to my parents. I think this mostly has to do with their desire to remain young themselves and their evasion and denial when it comes to old age.

The other day while I was rummaging through the attic for Halloween decorations I passed by a big brown folded corduroy jacket that had been my fathers when I was young. Before my parents moved here a few years ago, they had been sorting through old clothes and asked me if I wanted the weathered, old coat. I had packed it up to the attic and forgotten about it.

When I saw it, I picked it up and examined the dark, leather buttons and ran my fingertips along the wide wale of the cinnamon brown corduroy.

Instinctively, I buried my face into the folds of the aged, heavy, brown, knee- length coat. The scents filled my nostrils and I was transported in time. Immediately recalling the trapped fumes from the factory my father worked and the sweet aroma of peppermints, chewing gum and ink pens that had previously found transport in each pocket.

There is a certain smell that fathers have; I notice my husband has it, as well. Not quite an "odor" but a definite pheromone induced scent that leaves its mark on anything worn more than once. In fact, when my husband leaves town for work, I find myself snuggling up to his pillow and instantly feeling more at ease.

This momentary trip via nostril, brought back vivid memories of wandering into my parents bedroom and taking the coat from their bedside chair and wrapping myself up in it tightly after a hard day at school. When the security and smell of that jacket was all I needed to make me feel better.

My father is a big man. When I was young, I imagined that he was nine-feet tall and bullet proof. I would try on his shoes and coats and I remember I was so little that my arms stayed hidden inside the sleeves and my feet never left the arches of his brown leather Florshiems.

It was chilly in the attic as I looked through the boxes and I slipped the coat over my shoulders. I laughed when I found that I still couldn't reach my arms out of the sleeves forty years later.

I snuggled in the dusty old coat and let its heaviness fall onto my back and warm me while I searched the shelves. When I was done I placed it gently back on top of the old dresser where it was when I found it and gave it one more big sniff goodbye.

I suppose I could have it cleaned and packed into plastic and stored away. Preserved for posterity in cellophane and plastic wrap, but I won't.

Things like Daddy's jackets are meant to be used, snuggled and brought out on occasions to remember their purpose and their magic.

In fact, the next Christmas I visit the attic with my youngest in search of ornaments and Snowmen, I just might wrap her up in Papaws corduroy just to see how it fits.

Dads Favorite Cooked Cabbage

I can't remember where or when I first started making cabbage with beer. Perhaps it was on St. Patrick's Day one year, but there is something that beer, bacon and caramelized onions do to cabbage that takes it to a whole *nutha* level. Great when paired with Kielbasa or brats on the grill.

Ingredients:

One head of cabbage, cored, sliced and chunked.
1 onion sliced and diced
½ - ¾ pound bacon, diced.
½ stick of butter
1 beer, any kind.
In a large stock pot melt butter. Then stir in onion and bacon. Stir often and cook on medium heat until the onion is caramelized and the bacon begins to crisp. Do not drain. Toss in cabbage. Stir. Pour in one 12oz beer. Cover tightly with lid and cook on medium for 20 minutes. Stir once after 10 minutes. Replace lid. Serves 6.

Halloween, sugar comas and "Peeping Moms"

:~:~:~:~:~:~:~:~:~:~:~:~:

"No Spring nor summer beauty hath such grace, as I have seen in one autumnal face."
~John Donne

As Halloween arrives I always get a bit giddy. Just the smell of crisp leaves being crushed beneath my feet can flare my nostrils and transport me to a different time and place. I'm not sure what happens with that first foggy morning and seeing a little frost on that freshly carved pumpkin, but it sends me into a veritable Autumnal coma that lifts me up and carries me back to memories of wax wrapped candies, dark sidewalks crowded with goblins and staying out with my best friend Carol, until what seemed to be well after the 11:00 news.

It doesn't seem like my last Trick or Treat was nearly 35 years ago, but it was. I can remember each Halloween outfit, each candy filled pillow case and each night I went to bed with sticky sweet cheeks and a rumbly tummy full of sugary goodness.

When it came to choosing a costume, I always loved being inanimate objects brought to life through homemade materials, immortalized in felt or decked out in brown corduroy after a visit to my father's closet. I can still smell the well-worn jackets in my fathers closet; heavy with work fumes and faded scents Swisher Sweets cigars my mother insisted be smoked .

In the 70's when all my girlfriends were princesses and disco queens, I found myself donning my fathers shirt, a bandana on a stick with charcoal'd cheeks roaming the suburban streets as a hobo or cutting holes in my mothers favorite white twin Percale sheet as a ghost. I never pandered to the popular; instead I kept to the traditional haunts and costumes of yesteryear. That is, until I got older, when I became a felt green M&M, an Alka-Seltzer tablet complete with fizzy bubble headgear and even visited downtown bars in my twenties as a "bar-fly", which unfortunately more closely resembled a cockroach.

So it's no surprise for me to see two of our three children leaving the house this year as "Pinky" the Pac-Man ghost and a 5' 8" bright yellow Tetris block. Since our oldest son is nearly 18, he sits at home and gives out candy while the four of us scour the neighborhood looking for homes with glowing porch lights lit to declare their allegiance to the night.

It always surprises me how there are people that decorate their yards and houses in full Halloween Regalia and yet never seem to be home on the night of Trick or Treat.

It's almost like seeing an Open House sign and then finding the door locked. I always have to wonder if they had good intentions but fell asleep and missed the *witching hour* or if they are just Halloween Scrooges and enjoy tempting us with their fine decor'-Knowingly making plans to evade the delivery of sweet confections to wide-eyed children.

Each year we join the ranks of eager children roaming the neighborhood. Many with their *Peeping Tom* and *Gladys Cravitz* parents lingering in the shadows watching their Princes and Fairies hop from doorstep to doorstep all while trying to get a glimpse inside the doorway.

I'd be lying if I said I didn't enjoying taking a peek inside my neighbor's houses as we pass. I've always been a bit of a *Gladys*. I think deep down inside I just want to connect, see if their interior design skills are any indication of a commonality we can build on.

But then again it could be... I'm just nosey.

Beans n' Sweet Cornbread

Don't say it, because I won't hear of it. Now don't go telling me that you have never made beans or that you don't like them. I'm here to tell you that I've never met a bean I didn't like. It's all in the preparation.

Beans are a simple thing, really the most basic of foods. They can be done with little effort and their nutrition will stick to your ribs and make even the hungriest of men satiated. Packed with protein they are the Vegan's friend as well as the pocketbooks. The trick is finding that flavor where the bean still is a bean but the taste jumps off your tongue. You know you've found it when one bowl just isn't enough to satisfy your taste buds. Once you've found that happy combination of bean, cook time and pork, you've created a masterpiece and you're a proud member of the Beans n' cornbread club.

First and foremost choose your bean. Maybe you're brown bean folk, or Navy or perhaps the more pungent black bean is more to your liking. Whatever legume you choose, make sure that you do this; Soak your beans. This step is integral for flavor, decreasing foam and diminishing gas buildup in your lower intestine for the next 24 hours. This often missed, simple step can mean the difference between a nice flavorful soupy bean and an ugly foamy broth.

After you've selected your bean, go through your package of beans by hand and discard any stones or rubbish. Yes sometimes there are tiny stones in the beans. Toss them to the side and then place your selected beans in a large bowl and cover with 3 inches of water. Set them in the refrigerator for at least 6 hours, overnight is best.

Choose your meat. No beans are worth their salt if they don't have a little salt pork, bacon, jowl or country ham in 'em. Trust me, they need a swine inspired side kick or they just never reach their full potential.

My favorite pork to put in my beans is country ham *bits and pieces*. They are fairly cheap in price and you can buy them right next to the biscuit slices and the Country Ham steaks. These pork tidbits are the trimmings that were left after slicing and most of the time, they are more meaty than the more expensive cuts. You just have to take a minute and separate the pieces when you take them out of their package. Do NOT eat raw country ham. Yes, it smells delicious but it must be cooked in your beans first before consuming.

The "whole potato" used in this recipe will absorb the *"gas"* usually associated with soup beans. When placed in your pot of beans it will remove and absorb a great amount of the gas that would normally hide in the bean broth. While it is primarily an "old wives tale", I've found that it does work.

(But whatever you do, DO NOT eat that potato. You just might explode)

Ingredients:
1 small bag of dry beans. (Black, Navy, Pinto or Great Northern)
1 Small pkg Country ham pieces (or salt pork, jowl or thick sliced bacon)
1 diced onion
3 Bay leaves
1 potato (Peeled and Whole)

Directions:
1. Now that you've soaked your beans overnight, drain them through a strainer or colander. Spray them off with water and place them in a large stock pot.
2. Add fresh water to beans until beans are 2 inches below water line.
3. Add diced onion.
4. Add pork pieces.
5. Add Bay leaves and whole peeled potato.
6. Bring to a boil. Reduce heat to low/simmer and cover tightly.
7. Cook beans for 2 hours. Stirring frequently. If Beans get too thick add water 8 oz at a time.
8. Remove Bay leaves after simmering for 1 hour and remove whole potato. <u>DO NOT</u> eat this potato. Discard the potato and the Bay leaves.
9. After simmering for 2 hours, test the beans to see if they are tender. If so, you have made some great beans!

10. For Black Beans, after you have cooked the beans, remove ½ the beans and puree in food processor or blender. Then, return the pureed beans to the bean soup. This makes the entire dish easier to eat, adds a smooth texture and brings out the flavor of ham and bean in every bite.

Sweet Cornbread:
A good meal of soup beans is never complete without cornbread. Some prefer their cornbread dry and corny and some prefer it sweet. We prefer ours a little sweet with butter and honey on top.

Ingredients:
1 cup Self-Rising corn meal
1 cup flour
1/3 cup sugar
1 cup milk
1 large egg
1/ cup vegetable oil

Mix all ingredients in a bowl. Transfer to well greased skillet or pan and bake at 400* for 30 minutes. Cook until lightly browned on top. Serve with Soup beans and a big slap o' butter and a drizzle o' honey on top. This corn cake feeds 4.

My Mom Jeans Revolution Soundtrack
:~:~:~:~:~:~:~:~:~:~:~:

"We're fools whether we dance or not, so we might as well dance".
                              ~Japanese Proverb

Just when I thought I knew the real me, I go and find myself listening to Lil' Wayne and hip hop on my mp3 player while I get my housework done. Just when I thought I had found my music genre and my "life's soundtrack" I go and get a flip-side to myself.

Whodathunk?

Probably this is due to the fact that Creedence, Jimmy Buffet and James Taylor just don't give me that *"umph"* I need to maintain the frantic state of constant pick-up I need to get things done around here. I do know when the music slows down, I do too. So I have to maintain my groove 'til the last dish is in the washer, four beds are made and the floors are mopped.

I thought I had made it to my Jimmy Buffet and James Taylor years only to see that I am a revolving door of rhythm and music tastes. I find myself dialing up the sounds of Mary J., Lady Gaga, The Black Eyed Peas and Jay Z while dancing with my mop across the Pergo to the re-mix version of "I'm coming out" with Diana Ross joining in the chorus from the background. Of course along with my musical tastes changing I have to admit that lately I do feel more compelled to buy matching rims for my SUV and having a sippy-sippy of Hennessy doesn't seem like a bad idea either from behind my Prada sunglasses.

I used to believe I missed my mid-life crisis because I was too busy, but I now realize I was just on the cusp.

Seeing yourself clearly as a lady/child on the brink of full blown menopausal womanhood can bring you to your knees.

Thinking about time lost and no way to recapture it can make you gasp for air, go crazy and lose focus, even if you do now wear no line bi-focals. Awash in emotions you never knew you could have all at one time. Realizing that fun-loving gal behind that face in the mirror with the frown lines isn't the same one the world sees can cripple you if you let it.

But I am learning its okay to be me, regardless of what the world thinks and its okay that ol' Mama Rigney seems a bit wacky while she gets the laundry done-anyone who doesn't like it can do the laundry for me.

As dear old Popeye says, *"I yam what I yam"*.

Speaking of laundry, I don't know about the rest of you, but as an overweight woman I have the hardest time finding clothes. I am just not ready to surrender to the rounded necks and box shaped tops that define all women over forty. Being a round necked and box shaped woman myself, that certainly doesn't *"accentuate the positive"*.

Where are the cool clothes for the aged to perfection ladies? I certainly am not ready to surrender to *poly-want-some-cotton* shirts and "Mom Jeans" just yet. Regardless of my size, I am still eager to embrace that gal in me that appreciates clothes that match the mood I'm in. Clothes that don't look like burlap bags would be nice and shirts I don't have to avoid fall bonfires while wearing because of "flammable" caution tags in the collar.

I am not ready to go quietly into that good night of middle age.

I am not ready to succumb to all things polyester and elastic. I am all for comfort but can't it be pretty and unique even if it is available in every discount department store in America?

So join me in my attempt to step out of the box a bit, slip out of the norm and meet me on the sidelines for a dance during your work break or in between vacuuming and doing the dishes. Choose your life's soundtrack and change it often, don't cement yourself in the guidelines set by someone else before you. Sing, two-step or boogie-oogie-oogie your way into your forties and beyond.

I'm hoping that the next time I look in the mirror, I see that gal on the inside showing a bit more on the outside and don't be surprised if my frown lines fade a bit over the next few years instead of getting deeper, 'cause I got the music in me and I'm not afraid to let it show.

I'm not a good singer. In fact when I was younger I was what you call a "mouther" at church. You know the type, they open up their mouth during the hymns, *mouth* the words but no sound comes out. A silent echo of sorts. I was so sure I couldn't make a joyful noise that I just went through the motions to spare any unnecessary ear pain.

That all changed when we had our first child. For some reason, my made up songs about "itty bitty toes" and a "perty little nose" were welcomed with open ears and a sweet smile. A voice that I thought seemed annoying actually brought contentment to my "wee" one and much to my surprise gave me a certain sense of peace as well. Years passed, I had three children I had sung through their first colicky months of life with "homegrown" lullabies and now I was singing around the house all the time, with or without the kids in earshot. Life was good.

When it was time to don my apron and get some housework done, it seemed only natural to belt out a few old Elton John, James Taylor and Billy Joel hits without a care in the world-to the world or anyone that would listen. I think my kids know every James Taylor song by heart; I have mopped my way to "Carolina" through "fire and rain" too many times to count.

So a few years ago, when I had my thyroid removed because of cancer I found notes I had previously been able to reach were too much of a strain, so I stopped singing. I just quietly retired from my daily repertoire' and began using my mp3 player with headphones and listening to other people rejoice for me.

One afternoon, while "lip synching" a song to my mp3 player and loading the dishwasher, my oldest son asked me why I didn't sing anymore. I told him that my voice just wasn't the same. He said that it didn't matter, because the house seemed happier when I was singing and it seemed weird that it was so quiet and he didn't like it.

I guess over the years my singing had become an expression of love and joy and had nothing to do with the notes I hit or more often, missed.

My wee one, Lydia heard my son and I talking and rushed in throwing her arms around my waist and without hesitation and giving me a huge smile said, *"Mama, we love your singing, even if it does hurt our ears."*

After I stopped laughing, I realized I was wrong to omit something from my life that I enjoyed only because it wasn't the same as it used to be. Sometimes the desire to stop doing things you love because they change isn't always the best option, because you never know how much your actions may mean to someone else or to yourself.

When I feel sick or tired or *sick of being tired*, and things I am accustomed to are not the same for me, it's too easy to pretend they never existed and retreat under the covers. But that's not the person I need or want to be.

At various times in my life, I've had to do a personal inventory on my life. They've been extremely overdue inventories. There are times when I miss how easy things used to be and lately it can be overwhelming if I let it matter too much. I believe life is meant to be a bit rough as well as calm. Tempered with the easy and hard, sweet and sour and the climb after a fall is definitely worth the effort and you can't beat the view once you're back on top.

By realizing life isn't always perfect it's much easier to face each morning with a smile on my face, a song in my heart regardless of the melody, the soundtrack to my life is pretty good, even if it might send Aretha and Elton running for their earplugs.

"Sock it to me Cake"

Sock it to who? Sock it to me! This cake recipe came out in the 60's. The name was derived from a popular television variety show and it rose to the top quickly as a must-have for every baby shower, wedding rehearsal and teacher potluck.

Ingredients:
4 eggs
1 stick butter
½ Cup sugar
½ Cup of vegetable oil
1 box butter cake mix
8 oz sour cream
1 Cup of nuts (pecans, peanuts or walnuts)
1 tsp vanilla extract
Filling:
2 and ½ TBS brown Sugar
1 tsp cinnamon

Preheat oven to 375*. Mix all ingredients. Pour half of batter into well greased Bundt pan. Then top with 2 tablespoons of brown sugar and 1 tsp cinnamon. Add remaining batter. Bake 1 hour at 375*.

                        Moist and delicious!

The Terrible Fours, Fives and Forties
:~:~:~:~:~:~:~:~:~:~:~:

Our third child Lydia entered this world kicking and screaming and continued to do so for five years. We have come so far, and I wanted other mothers that have a temperamental angel like mine to understand that it does get better. We all survived. She finally became more comfortable with the world and has come full circle into a well-adjusted young lady.

I never thought I would be afraid of one of our children. But my third made me a poster child for nerve disorders and stress eating. I always assumed that since we had successfully brought two boys out of their preschool years without too much emotional scarring for any of us, that we surely could handle our third child Lydia, who turns 10 this July.

There were times as an infant and toddler when she was angelic and I came very close to relaxing, then she would do something so unexpected that watching her was like watching a train derail. I could see her start on a path where she was destined for sorrow, but she rarely detoured and continued her hell bent journey, regardless of the consequence.

I was not raised with a "time-out chair". I'm told by my parents, that I was a pretty good child. I was born in 1963, I had two sisters that were ten years older, so my parents were busy just dealing with that entire decade of weirdness. There were a few times I am sure I sat in the corner, but for the most part, I just went with the flow of things and realized that there were some things I had to live with whether I liked them or not.

My daughter's stubbornness began when she was about a year old, and did not want to go to bed. She learned to force herself to throw up in her crib, so I would have to go in and clean her up. Her doctor said that it was a very smart child that managed to master that ability and unfortunately it would take a strong will on my part to get through it. That was a long, pine-sol scented, month.

Afterwards, I felt so good that I had managed to outsmart her. But then, feeling empowered by being more intelligent than my 12 month old made me feel flippin' ridonculous. Over the next five years she managed to disrupt our house on a daily basis. Her main dialogue was whining or crying. It became so intense that I took her to the doctor and requested they look deeper into her "psyche" but they returned with the facts that I already knew, she was perfectly healthy, mentally and physically, she was just strong willed, very determined, and more rested than the rest of us.

When she was around five and told her brother that he was a *"stupidhead"*, after repeated corrections, I finally dropped a tiny bit of foamy soap on her tongue to "wash out" her mouth. I told her that if she continued to use mean words we would have to do it again and I asked her what she thought about her consequence. She looked at me with those big beautiful blue eyes and replied with full honesty, "*I think I want soap with flavor*".

Her frank response brought a smile to my face and I turned my head so she wouldn't see. After all, this was intended to break a bad habit, not test the palatability of liquid Dial. But it did bring about a new perspective for me, and I realized that one day her spunk and her determination may serve her well in this world that constantly tries to break the spirit of so many. Although she is testing her limits here at home, it makes me proud that she is a free thinker, and in the long run that may be what pushes her ahead of trouble. Or at the very least scares everyone out of her path.

Through all of our ups and downs, Lydia has brought an immense amount of purpose to my life. Being a mother of a newborn at nearly forty was exhausting. Each day that she managed to fuss less and smile more, I felt better about myself. Every time she gives her brothers a hug or bows her head in prayer I feel better about life. Watching her do the right thing when she doesn't know I am there, shows our hard work has made a difference.

When all is said and done, I know David and I are doing our best. I know she will one day be a very strong woman that I will need to lean on later. The child that I had thought would break me has instead taught me to bend and I've become only slightly *cracked* in the process.

Carolyn Rigney's Greek Pot Roast

First things first, if you don't own a crock pot, stop reading immediately and go buy one. I can't imagine my life without this ceramic godsend. This recipe is from my mother in law, Carolyn. If she wasn't family, she'd be my friend anyway. I loved her as soon as we met.

ONLY 2 Ingredients!
1. 3-4 lb. Beef pot roast. (Chuck, Round, Sirloin tip any cut will do)
2. 12 oz. jar of Greek Pepperoncinis. NOT hot peppers, just the green or golden Pepperoncinis found in the pickle section of the supermarket.

Directions:
Plug in the crock pot.
Place on HI setting.
Drop in your Beef roast, fat side down. No need to sear first or trim fat.
Pour the ENTIRE jar of Pepperoncinis on top of roast including juice. DO not stir. Place lid securely on top. DO NOT OPEN FOR 6 hours. NO PEEKING.

I usually cook it for 6-7 hours for a large roast, 'til that sucker is falling apart with a fork. It will be perfectly seasoned, not pickled, just a bit of heat on the taste buds. Most kids even love it. Mine do. First night I serve the roast with rice, a side of green vegetable and a salad. Night #2 its shredded in tortillas with a green tomatillo sauce or salsa and a side of beans and leftover rice. This is a no brainer and it makes a great impression on those guests that think you can't cook.

De-Evolution of Resolutions
:~:~:~:~:~:~:~:~:~:~:~:

"A New Year's resolution is something that goes in one Year and out the other." ~Anonymous

My yearly New Year's resolution from now on... no resolutions.

I resolve to not make any I can't keep anyway. I know that my twisted road of life is paved with them, and most of them have always been so extreme that I used them as punishment for my inadequacies. Sometimes I think we all do that. My past resolutions have included my view of myself as too fat, too judgmental, too stressed, too angry, too busy, too fat, too lazy and did I mention, too fat?

For some reason, announcing to the world that I am overweight is my way of making myself wake up and rise to the occasion of weight loss, exercise and self deprecation. The past year I managed to lose over thirty pounds only to pack on twelve during the holidays. But I am sure I am not alone in that club. I love eating. In fact, my love affair with food has been a lifelong relationship. It has helped me in the best of times and the worst of times. I could blame food for the fact I am overweight, but it would be like blaming a flame for being hot. It is what it is, sometimes nourishing me and sometimes just satisfying a need but still a necessity to survive. You can't quit eating "cold turkey" and chalk it up to a past vice, and forget about it. Well I suppose you could, it's called starvation and it doesn't have a very good outcome or a long term prognosis. So for me, I just have to accept I love eating, choose the right things and get over the psychoanalysis of why I feel the need to consume to console.

My son asked me recently, *"What would happen if you just stopped dieting and ate normally? Why do you need to diet?"*

It took me a few minutes and I was pleased at my epiphany so I answered him honestly, *"Well, if I stop dieting, if I stop denying myself, how else will I punish myself for being fat?"*

My son looked at me and we both let this thought sink in. He and I both knew I had come to terms with myself in that moment. In that moment I fully understood that my dieting isn't a way to fix myself, but to punish myself. An interior beating of the psyche. I had become my own bully.

Getting back to my newly unveiled view of resolutions...For some reason, I have always felt the need to discuss my shortcomings over my achievements; it seems I have always done that. I was always told nobody likes a braggart and then ran with that philosophy.

"Hello, my name is Margie. Lover of food, eater of feelings and confessor of sins."

Of course it's not always easy to be someone that is willing to disclose their most delicate of secrets, their deepest fears and their biggest faults, but maybe it makes me more at ease by admitting I am not superwoman. But it also makes me more vulnerable and believe it or not, I actually like that. Once I realized that I don't have to be superwoman or live up to some unrealistic picture of a mother and/or woman that I can never achieve, it sure does make it easier on the spirit and the family I live with. Unfortunately, there are millions of women and men out there beating themselves up daily for not being perfect, when in reality; imperfection is in itself the art of being human.

It really is a shame we have allowed the media to put so much emphasis on what the outside of our bodies should look like. Little girls and boys are growing up with some freaky looking air-brushed role models with very little to offer in the way of moral character or intelligence. I am so thankful for the grounded sense of self my parents gave me and the fact that I didn't grow up during a time of mass media coverage of all things svelte, skinny and silicone. When I was growing up, if your underwear was visible above your pants or you had giant droopy jeans-people would assume you were intellectually and/or financially challenged.

Tattoos were fake, boobs were real and we all wished Mayberry was our hometown and Carol Brady was our mother.

Television bombards us each January with advertisements for diet plans and equipment for rapid weight loss. Some say they provide your meals for you so that you don't have to plan them, some are pills to enhance your dieting experience, some are shakes and some are exercise equipment that resembles torture devices and apparatus I have seen in science fiction films. All of them look promising, but none of them include will-power, motivation or desire. Until you have those, you will most likely end up with UPS delivered appetizers, unused vitamins and a two thousand dollar home gym that doubles for a coat rack.

Maybe instead of making resolutions a yearly event, we should make them a part of our lives daily. Then, if we mess up, we just brush ourselves off and start all over again the next morning. No harm, no foul - an official "do-over" with no points taken away for poor performance.

That sure sounds good to me and maybe I won't have to motivate myself for weeks to prepare for my next attempt at the treadmill and salad bar.

And it's better than ordering tasteless frozen food in the mail and sweatin' my arse off to the "Oldies" alone in my living room.

Aunt Louise's (Inza's) 7 layer salad

My Aunt Louise is a lovely woman. She always treated me like a third daughter when I was young. Her home and her house was a place I could call a second home and her cooking was inspirational. She could entertain two complete sides of her family and never miss a beat from soup to nuts she could cater a meal and end it with a bounty of desserts.

This recipe is one she perfected over time and I think it is the best cure for a Summer meal that needs a kick start. Frozen peas and Parmesan cheese along with the crunch of fresh cauliflower will make this a pleasing meal by itself or as a compliment to grilled burgers. Making it a day ahead is integral in incorporating the flavors.

Ingredients:
1 Head of lettuce. (Cored and chopped)
1 Head of cauliflower. (Washed and separated into bite size pieces)
1 package of cooked, crumbled bacon
1 small bag of frozen green peas
1 and ½ cups of Parmesan cheese (shredded or granulated)
6-8 Green onions, chopped.
1 ½ cups of Mayonnaise (Aunt Louise says that only Hellman's will do-but I have used others)

1. In an oblong dish make a 2 inch layer of lettuce. Then top with a layer of cauliflower. Follow this with layered dollops of Mayo. Smooth out mayonnaise to cover the area completely. 2. Add a layer of frozen peas.
3. Sprinkle on Parmesan cheese, green onions and top with bacon.
4. Cover with plastic wrap and allow dish to sit in refrigerator overnight. Before serving, allow salad to sit for 15 minutes at room temperature.

King of the Lawn Boys
:~:~:~:~:~:~:~:~:~:~:

"Oh the times they are a' changin"...Isn't that how the old Bob Dylan song goes?

It certainly is true, the times are changing. It seems like just yesterday I was just getting engaged. Now, here I am over twenty years later, married, mothering and mortgaged.

I see how far my husband David and I have come, and it seems like our life is in fast forward now. Times that seemed only a distant dream have come and gone. Pregnancies that seemed would never end have produced three children that are growing so quickly we can't keep them in proper fitting shoes.

We're in our third house and I'm not sure it will be our last. We're even on our third dog. I forget how many cars and vans we've had, but I am happy to say that we've only had two mowers. I remember my father had three, all at the same time. When one wouldn't start or remain started, he could quickly put another in its place. Sometimes, he used all three mowers in one afternoon, and this was just in their yard in suburbia.

My father certainly was proud of his mower collection. I know that some people looked at them as junk. But the mere fact that he could keep them running (even though to the naked eye they seemed like junkyard fodder) gave him a sense of power over his neighbors *"one pull start"* gems.

There was a certain air of mastery when he, and only he, could get the most elderly of the Lawn Boys to rev up, as if he were the best cowboy on the ranch, and he was the only one that could tame the newest wild Mustang.

Now, those days of the lawnmower militia are gone for my father. Time has stood still for none of us, and he only owns one mower now, one that is in top condition and starts with a turn of a key. Even though, now he isn't the one doing the mowing my oldest son William is.

It's hard to sit and watch from the front row as your parents begin the fourth quarter of their lives. Especially knowing I am fast approaching the third quarter of my own. Still, I don't see myself as aging on the inside, I feel as though I am still twenty years old only bound to an aging body that sometimes forsakes me.

I can't remember the last time I ran through an overgrown field, but I still know exactly how it feels to have the blades of grass whipping at my knees. I think sometimes it's easy to forget our parents may not be able to do the things we talk about, but they still understand and remember how youth feels.

When I was small my Grandfather was too ill to throw a ball with me, but he would share stories of his youth and speak with such detail that it felt like I was there too, peeking over his shoulder seeing it just as clearly as the day it happened.

Sometimes when one of my children tells me about a bad day at school, I try to console them by telling them I had those same days, and they often look at me like I have no idea how they feel. I probably did the same when my Mother empathized with me.

Lately, I find myself saying things I swore as a child I would never say to my own. *"Because I said so"* were the most hated four words of my childhood. It's hard to look at myself in the mirror after I hear those words come out of my mouth, even harder to see how easily it happens.

It's funny how the things I used to make fun of my mother for doing, I find myself doing. I used to think it was so funny that she would call my sisters and I by the wrong name, and even funnier when my father combined our names into one "new" name, like "Marleesa", which was a mixture of Margie, Marsha and Lisa. My sisters and I had a good laugh when Mom would forget where she put something, or the one time she sprayed furniture polish on her hair instead of hairspray. That doozy was epic. Nobody messed with my mothers hair. Because she put so much effort into protecting her "do" all week.

We have a lot of good memories because of my mothers mid life mistakes. One time, she caught a wok on fire because she had the burner on too high, and my father threw it out the back door like a flaming flying saucer. I don't think she ever used it again because we teased her so much.

These days, I don't find it as funny when I can't find my keys and they're still in the front door, when I burn the biscuits because I forget they're in the oven, or when I get frantic because I can't find my purse and it's on my shoulder.

So, I guess in a way, the times aren't really changing, they're just rearranging. Silently moving from one generation to the next, making each of us see life from someone else's shoes, even if the shoes just don't seem to fit.

Dump Cake

Even though the name may sound a bit odd, this is the easiest, most tasty way to feed that sweet tooth you've been starving because you think you don't have time to make something delicious. As long as there has been cake mix and canned pie filling, there has been Dump Cake.

Ingredients:
1 – 20 oz. can of cherry pie filling
1 – 20 oz. can of crushed pineapple (in juice or syrup)
1 – box of yellow cake mix (any brand)
1 – 7 oz. pkg. of shredded coconut (optional)
2/3 cup chopped pecans (optional)
2 sticks of butter

1. In a greased oblong glass dish "dump" the following.
2. First dump in the cherry pie filling and spread evenly.
3. Then dump in the pineapple and juice evenly.
4. Open cake mix and sprinkle entire box across pineapple/cherry layers.
5. (optional step) add coconut and/or pecans.
6. Slice butter into ¼ inch slices and layer across top of cake mix evenly. It should look like tiny window panes.
7. Bake at 350* for one hour. Do not burn or overcook.

Enjoy! It's very similar to a cobbler and you can substitute the pie filling for any flavor combination. Great with vanilla ice cream on top.

"Son" Shine on my Shoulders
:~:~:~:~:~:~:~:~:~:~:~:~:

"A baby is God's opinion that the world should go on"
~Carl Sandburg

It's hard for me to believe that William, my oldest has turned eighteen years old. I can't believe that this 6'2" man/child was ever small enough to fit in my arms. Just yesterday his little head would rest on my shoulder after a burping and fall asleep, leaving a small crusty remnant of his last meal there. I remember the first six months of his life I smelled baby formula whenever I turned my head. I wore those little stains with pride. I considered it an honor to have this child. This tiny token of love that God had given us to raise.

When William was born, he was considered a miracle to me as he was preceded by a brother that only made it through the second trimester of my first pregnancy. Each day I was pregnant with William was filled with caution and I was aware of every kick, turn and hiccup. I cherished every moment and every day that he greeted me with a kick to the ribs or a jab to the kidneys.

My husband Dave would rub my belly and call to him *"Willie, this is your Daddy, I know you're in there"*…and we never knew for sure what the sex of any of our children would be, but we just felt he was a William, and indeed he was.

He arrived after what seemed days of labor, red faced and hungry. He taught me how to be a mother. I owe all I am as a mother to my children. There are no instruction booklets that prepare you for parenting. They may write books, but nothing prepares you for that first look into your baby's eyes when you know that you are in charge and have been given this awesome responsibility of caring for Gods greatest creation. I actually felt a bit unworthy of such precious life. Was God sure I could handle this?

The first weeks, I wondered. William had a bit of colic and fought breast feeding because he wanted the feeling of a full belly. So we switched to bottle feeding and he was immediately at ease. His belly could be full, he was satiated and happy. All was well.

Time that Dave and I used to spend watching TV was now spent watching William for hours each evening. We waited for every milestone to hit, the rolling over, the belly crawls and then finally standing up on his own. With each phase, William went for it with fervor. He went from toddling to running immediately. He was a powerhouse. Up and down the hall he would run, back and forth over and over without tiring and just watching him was exhausting. Moving those tiny legs on his wagons, ride alongs and before we knew it he was riding a bike without training wheels around the court before his 5th birthday.

We used to laugh at him on his tiny bike that he adored. He was just 4 years old and already his legs were too long for his beginner bike. He looked like a bear riding a trike in the circus…legs all bent up to his chin, but he loved that bike and would not trade up until the treads finally wore through the tires.

Now he has traded his bicycles for car keys. I get behind the wheel of our Earth Destroyer 9000 and have to move the seat up 5 inches to reach the brakes after he has been in the driver's seat. I have to adjust the mirrors and it's a reminder of how much he has grown in just 18 years, from that tiny baby to this *beanpole* of a man. Sometimes I sit there from his perspective for just a moment and let the reality of time sink in. How fast it has all come to this point; where boyhood meets manhood and the inevitable adult milestone is reached.

All those times when I would be anxious for him to sleep through the night, walk on his own, have more independence from me, I now wish I hadn't rushed. To do it all again I would do gladly. The good, the bad and the sleepless nights but maybe I would cherish them a bit more, breathe them in a bit deeper and appreciate more of the small things. How his hand would fit in mine, how his toes resembled peas all nesting up against one another, how sweet the back of his neck smelled and how he looked at me like I was his world, when in reality he was mine.

So for this Mama seeing my son turn 18 is bittersweet. But I am so proud of the man he has become. He is sweet and kind, funny and intelligent. He still shows me how to be a better parent every day by being such a wonderful son. He walked out of November as a man to the rest of the world, but to me he will always be.....my baby boy.

Favorite Broccoli Casserole

Broccoli sure has come into greater popularity over the years, but I still can't seem to get my son Benjamin to appreciate it's importance to the human body. But for the rest of us, we love this dish. Thanksgiving, Christmas or any big meal, has to have Broccoli Casserole or it's just not a meal. My daughter will tell anyone that listens this is her favorite food. She used to draw crayon pictures of it in kindergarten when they had to draw their favorite things. You gotta love a gal that knows good food...

Ingredients:
½ large Vidalia or sweet onion (diced)
4 stalks celery (diced)
½ stick butter
1 can of cream of mushroom soup
1 can of cream of chicken soup
½ cup of Mayonnaise
2 bunches of fresh Broccoli
2 cups of cubed Velveeta
½ pkg saltine crackers
½ stick of butter

In a microwave safe dish, place ½ stick of butter, diced celery and diced onion. Cook on HI in microwave for 1 minute. Let stand.

In a large pot bring enough water to boil to cook two bunches of fresh broccoli. Add broccoli and cook until *"almost"* done.

Drain Broccoli. Cut into bite size pieces.

In a large mixing bowl, add broccoli, cooked onion, celery and melted butter, both cans of soup, Mayonnaise, diced cheese and stir well.

Pour mixture into well greased large oblong glass dish.
Crumble Saltines fine and sprinkle on top.
Place cut butter pats of ½ stick of butter on top and bake at 350* until bubbly and lightly browned on top.

mmm...mmm...good. In the words of my father, Bill Miller;

"Tastes so good, you'll have to tie a string 'round your tongue to keep from swallowin' it."

Sweet scents and toddling toes
:~:~:~:~:~:~:~:~:~:~:~:~:
"Life is what happens while you are making other plans."
~John Lennon

One fall afternoon, I tripped over something in the back of the closet while changing items from the front to the back and noticed the carrying case of our old Sony handi-cam movie camera and decided to peruse our video collection and begin the transfer to DVD all the movies that we had of the kids, per David's expertise with all things electronic.

I had forgotten the contents of most of them and some of them were never viewed after they were taken. We just put them away and took it for granted that tomorrow would come and we would look at them then. Then, tomorrow came and left and the camera stayed in its case, quietly in the dark, placing second to our new digital camera.

As soon as the first tape was popped in, our previous life began to unfold on the television and I was swept into this alternate world, this past that I had forgotten and took all too much for granted.

There he was in full Technicolor, my little Benjamin Russell, our second son, toddling with his soft blonde baby hair swaying in the breeze as he danced to tunes of Barney and Elmo playing in the background. When Benjamin was born, the nurse handed him to me after a few hours in her care, and she said, *"He's going to be an easy one"*...she must have been a psychic, but she was right, he truly is just as easy as he can be.

Looking at him nearly full size on the television screen I could almost smell the sweetness of his skin. I longed to hold his little body in my arms again.

Ahh...Baby smell. If there is one scent I wish I could revisit it would be the heavenly scent that used to reside at the nape of my children's necks as babies. That sweet scent trapped just below the hairline that I loved to bury my face in and inhale all that was baby Rigney.

That is the sweetest perfume that ever existed, that mixture of newborn and pheromone. Its very core was near angelic in nature and seemed to originate from the clouds of heaven itself. As if my children had resided there prior to showing up in my arms and the scent of God and honesty was still fresh on their skin.

I like to think that is what innocence, goodness and purity smell like. This is probably why no adults have it and it disappears so quickly.

Benjamin was the sweetest of babies. I can almost feel how warm his little hands were as they rested on my leg before he would lay his head down on my lap to show me he was sleepy. I sat there, drawn into this world and felt a melancholy longing I did not even know existed. How could I have forgotten how cute he looked as he danced, or how he scrunched up his little nose when he wanted to make us laugh? How did I forget how excited and animated William was and how mesmerized Lydia could be as she tap-danced the hours away to her reflection in the oven door?

I was compelled to watch for the hours it took to make the transfer over the next three days at two hour intervals. For 120 minutes a session, I was transported through time into the living room of what felt like a past life, a visit to a world that I felt still existed even though in reality it was no longer there. Through the magic of film I could feel the textures and hear the sounds of our previous home and our simple life, where most of our focus was centered on sippee cups, favorite blankies and the comfort of a clean diaper.

Looking at these images I am reminded of how uncomplicated our lives used to be, before the economic landslide, my thyroid cancer, middle school and aging parents. It seems like in just in a small amount of time, even though I am wiser, I have also become more jaded. Less likely to fall for the obvious and in that process not as open to the possibilities that life holds by already knowing the outcome of unopened doors and roads less traveled.

If it were possible, would I want to go back and repeat these years I have on tape? The answer is undoubtedly yes, to smell the sweetness of my children as newborns and to caress their tiny hands and feet once again, I would gladly make the trip. Just to hold them again for the "first" time would be so wonderful, except this time, maybe I would try harder to hold on to that moment and not be so worried about the next.

What a pity we don't have a replay button in real life. What a shame when we make mistakes that we can't take them back or correct hurt feelings or regret. I suppose if there is one lesson I have learned it is one I find myself often repeating, that life and childhood are precious and much too short.

I remember thinking when I was in my teens how slow life was, how it seemed like I was constantly waiting to turn one year older, now I want to slow down the clock and rest where I am, grabbing for whatever I can hold on to so I can savor the moment just a bit longer, the emotion a bit deeper and the love a bit stronger.

After I watched all the home movies, I looked at my children a bit differently. Not as the eighteen year old eating machine, the fourteen year old perpetual-gaming king and the ten year old gotta-have-it-now Wee One, but instead I saw children who are forever my children, forever my babies regardless of how much they grow. I am so grateful I had this chance to relive that part of our lives together once again.

Eventually they will all mature, move out and have families of their own and when they do, I can always turn to my dvd's to a time of how things used to be, when life was simple, sweet and we were all...

Forever young.

Kentucky Burgoo
"Burgoooooo".

It's even fun to say. If you've never heard of Burgoo, just ask someone from the Bluegrass state and they'll tell you that creating this dish is a culinary art. Comprised of local meats and vegetables, this hearty stew will feed an army and leftovers freeze easily and even taste better the next day. A big whoppin' stock pot of Burgoo is popular as a Thoroughbred Race Season dish as well as the anchor for wakes, reunions and holiday gatherings.

Not for the faint of heart and not for tree-huggers and vegetarians, this dish needs meat and plenty of it.

Originally this dish contained any meat available. The original Kentucky Hunters Stew. Consisting, but not limited to, squirrel, mutton, deer, chicken, grouse, Elk, pork and beef. Since the majority of those meats are hard to find for the suburban cook I choose Beef, pork and chicken as my primary meats and the adaptation tastes just fine. However I am including five meats just so you can have a full authentic recipe to go by, just substitute the meats by the pound if you choose to omit any.

This is a nearly all day affair. You are united with your kitchen for a journey that will unfold from late lunch 'til the dinner hour. What you have ahead of you will create a mouth watering scent that will linger in your home for days.

First. Get a huge pot. I have a speckled blue and white canning pot I use, because I make this dish 3-5 gallons at a time. I serve it at Christmas and Fall parties. It's a complete meal in a bowl and it satisfies the most hard-core carnivores.

Ingredients for Burgoo:
2-3 pound beef chuck roast
1 – 2 pounds lamb (shoulder is best)
1 large ham bone
1 whole chicken about 3 lbs. (fryer, stewing or roasting hen)
1 small pork roast (1 -2 lb)

In a large stock pot, place all meats and "just" cover with water, then season with some salt and pepper. Bring to a boil, then reduce heat to simmer and cook until meat is tender and easy to remove from the bones. Stir often so there is no sticking or burning.

When fully cooked, remove meats and reserve "broth". Take skin, fat and bones from the meat. Return the shredded and cut meat to the reserved broth.

To your large pot of broth and meat add the following:
½ bunch celery (1/4 inch slices or chopped)
½ pound carrots (sliced ¼ inch or chopped)
3-4 green peppers (chopped)
3 sweet onions (chopped)
1 ½ pounds frozen or canned green beans (drained)
5 medium white potatoes (peeled, diced)
1 head of cabbage (chopped and/or shredded)
1 small bag of frozen peas
1 16 oz bag of Frozen (not breaded) Okra (this may not be your favorite veggie but it is vital to the taste of the Burgoo and the authenticity is incomplete without this under appreciated vegetable)
1 16 oz bag of frozen corn
3-4 15 oz cans of Whole or Diced Tomatoes (with juice)
6 oz of Worcestershire sauce
1 small bottle or 10 oz. of Tomato ketchup
1/3 cup of white vinegar
4 Bay Leaves

Cook all vegetables and meat until vegetables are tender and broth is thickened. If broth is still to thin add 2/3 cup of instant mashed potatoes. Remove Bay leaves.

After cooking is complete pour in 1 cup of good burgundy wine and stir. Serve in bowls with yeast rolls or hearty fresh bread slices. Some people serve this over rice or mashed potatoes, but I prefer it as is, in all its heavy bodied glory.

"Because I Said So"
:~:~:~:~:~:~:~:~:

"When I have kids, I'm not gonna treat them like you do me, I'm gonna be their friend and let them do whatever they want."
~age, 15 (me)

Wow, what a liar I was. I can still remember telling my mother that big speech in the living room of our old house when I was the ripe old age of fifteen; Hands on hip, all matter-of-fact and full of *"just you wait and see"*. I could just imagine how cool I would be as a parent and how much my own kids would adore me because I was fun and easy and let them do all the things I was wishing my parents would let me do at that time. Wishing my "future self" was my own mother and allowing me to stay out late and be independent of them, while still being able to access money that I needed for movies, eating out and fun.

I also remember my mother nearly smiling at my declaration, and responding with, *"Oh really? You just wait and see Margie May...you just wait and see"*.

Man o man, was she right. It's amazing how many things I say now that my mother said to me as a child, that I swore I would never repeat. *"Because I said so"* are probably the 4 most hated words in the universe to a child. Nothing trumps that. No words can be expressed to change their mind once those words are spoken by a Mom or Dad, it is the beginning and the end, the alpha and the omega, the first and last words you will hear - the subject is officially-dead.

My sisters and I didn't argue with our parents much. They were steadfast. From early on, we knew that our father meant what he said. He was ex-military and we all knew the drill. Ask him once and he would *"think about it"* but ask again too soon and it was always *"No"*. Dad liked to be asked once and then he would give you an answer later. Begging him for anything would always result in a *"I told you not to ask me again, so the answer is now- No."* Which was heartbreaking, if you could, you felt like physically beating the doo

doo out of yourself because you knew better, wishing you could turn back time and kept your mouth shut.

I remember one time, my sister slammed her bedroom door and she came home the next day to find my Dad carrying her door to the basement. He said he was tired of hearing it slam and now she couldn't do it anymore. So she went a while with no door. Of course my other sister would step in and out of her doorway threshold just to annoy her. I don't think any of us slammed anymore doors and she eventually got her door back.

My father liked to think he made most of the decisions when my sisters and I were young, but in actuality my mother made most of them. He was the "head of the family" but she was the "neck" and she could turn his head in any direction she wanted without him even knowing. Most of the time she just let him think he was in charge but we all knew better. Once we figured that out, we presented our cases to Mom and she would "lobby" for us, she was very subtle.

Now that I am a parent, I find myself doing and saying so many of the things I swore as a child I would never do or utter. I even have many of the characteristics of my father, which surprises me. I have even used the "*ask me again and the answer is no*" trick. You know why? Because it works! Plus it gives me some time to really evaluate what is going on since I feel like I am going in three different directions. Sometimes I don't feel like the "head" or the "neck" of the family. I'm just bringing up the "rear".

Our children are eighteen, fourteen and nine. Spread way too far apart to have any of them going through the same stages at the same time, which is both a blessing and a curse. Just when I think I am done with one phase that nearly broke me, I have two more *tours of duty* to look forward to.

We always joke that our oldest son William is our "test child" we all learn from his mistakes. The other kids and David and I have honed our skills by watching him. Now that he is 18 and we can see him becoming a remarkable young man, we find ourselves quietly celebrating, but afraid to get too excited as we realize there are most tests to come he isn't finished with us yet.

A few years ago, I came up with some house rules for us all to try and live by. I am sure I did this after some war or terror that was laid out by one of the kids in an attempt to brainwash them by printing them out, framing them and hanging them in one of our bathrooms. Hoping while they were searching for "reading material" they would subliminally succumb to their righteousness.

When we had our previous house for sale, one of the prospective buyers asked our realtor after reading our list of rules, "*Does anybody really live like this?*" To which I would like to publicly reply,

"No, but wouldn't it be nice?"

Here is a copy of our "house rules", if you've ever used our guest bathroom, you already know them. These rules are *broken* probably more than they are followed, but we Rigneys are a work in progress...

*<u>**Rigney House Rules:**</u>*
No hitting, No yelling.
We are all a family here.
We all have feelings.
Think first, be kind.
Don't yell it, tell it.
Don't do the crime,
if you can't do the "time".
Accept responsibility.
Learn from your mistakes.
Don't be a blamer, be a claimer.
Live in Peace, and try not to go to pieces.
God loves you and you are important.
In this house, You matter.
Love,
Mama and Dad

Believe it or not, I think it may have done some good. Because these rules have been quoted to me a few times when the kids remind me that I broke one of 'em, I suppose that's a good sign. That means they read them. Who knows? Maybe I'll finally learn to obey a few of them too.

'Nilla Front Porch Tea

While most people love sweet tea, this is a tea that pushes the palate a bit further with hints of vanilla and almond. It's the perfect beverage for a swing on the porch in the heat of summer or taking a picnic down by the creek. It cools, satisfies and makes merry the most mundane of hot summer days.

Ingredients:
6 Tea Bags (orange Pekoe, Red or Black tea)
5 cups boiling water
4 cups cold water
1 ½ tsp almond extract
1 ½ tsp Vanilla extract
1 and 2/3 cups sugar
2/3 cup lemon juice

1. Place sugar, lemon juice and tea bags in a large heat resistant pitcher. Pour 5 cups of boiling water over these ingredients. Place lid on pitcher and wait while it steeps for about 20 minutes. Remove tea bags and discard.
2. Add cold water, vanilla extract and almond extract.
3. Stir.
4. Serve over ice in tall glasses and garnish with thin slices of orange or a sprig of fresh mint from the garden.

Best Friends and Breadsticks
:~:~:~:~:~:~:~:~:~:~:

A good friend is a connection to life - a tie to the past, a road to the future, the key to sanity in a totally insane world. ~Lois Wyse

Although I turn 48 this year; one hot Tuesday afternoon in July at a quiet Italian eatery in downtown Lexington, I was 22 again.

Four college friends and I gathered around giant breadsticks slathered in butter and garlic. For a few hours we put our diets, work, ringtones and stress on hold. We committed this time to sharing our lives, photos and stories that have transpired over the past twenty five years. Smiles, laughter and hugs were in abundance and spirits were lifted high above the rafters of that old converted church awash in the heavenly scents of oregano and parmesan.

With the help of pictures to stir up old memories, we reconnected, reminisced and relaxed. There were moments where I laughed so hard my sides hurt and there were times where I held back a few tears.

I had to ask myself how I ever let these women slip from my life? How people so attached could move on without holding hands and marching boldly into the future? Together. Arm in arm. Telling the world it belonged to us and helping one another pick up the pieces when it obviously didn't. I asked these questions and yet I already knew the answers, I knew that indeed that was how it is meant to be. That we surround ourselves with people that help us become who we are, then let ourselves wander from them, stepping out on our own only to return when we are able to appreciate the relationship for all it is and all it was, in all it's glory.

It's not easy to think of myself as over forty and even harder to imagine myself near fifty. In fact, I just choked a little bit writing that last part and I may need to excuse myself for a minute.

During our luncheon, cameras were retrieved from purses and placed on the table. Lying in wait, like a cat ready to pounce on an unsuspecting mouse. Suddenly I was aware that I shouldn't have worn my white shirt, black would definitely have made me look thinner, but too late...a "click" and a "*smile!*" and I was forever immortalized in my embroidered mother-earth gauzy tunic and white jean shorts. The latter of which made me look as if I had marshmallows in my gene pool.

I like being behind the lens not in front of it. I think the reason I hate having my picture taken, aside from the obvious, is that it's photographic proof that I am aging as well as pushing the limits on my Lee jeans comfort-fit waistband. Because inside, I still feel young and fit, outside...not so much. This body has been through four surgeries and two doses of radiation in just over a year. I have now become the physical manifestation of the term "not aging well"; A term which only the girls that peaked early at my high school have been previously privy to.

Seeing photos of myself not only twenty-five years younger but nearly sixty pounds lighter was like seeing myself in another lifetime, revisiting a time that I had forgotten even existed and it was good for me. It was good for all of us and it made me realize that I am still that young girl lying on a beach towel unashamed, I am still that college girl in a toga wearing a twin-bed sheet with sprigs of shrub in her hair and I am still that young mother holding her newborn. I am just in a different package.

My mother who just turned 80 this year, told me in a quiet moment as I buckled her seatbelt before I drove her to the hairdresser, "*You know, I see my body and I know it looks older on the outside, I know that is all some people see, but inside, I still feel the same inside, just like I did when I was in my twenties*".

I didn't think that much about it when she said it. But later, when I had a moment to sit I realized how similar we all are as we age. We reach out to capture those things about ourselves that make us who we are, without losing who we've become. We want the world to see us not only on the outside but on the inside too.

I imagine that in *vehicular* terms, I am the dependable family car.

Not quite the antique and definitely not a brand new model. There is no "new car scent" lingering in any of my upholstery. Most assuredly I'm a four-door and perhaps even an SUV with a third row seat; Easy to drive, but hard on gas.

I am thankful for my reunion and glad I reconnected with a certain brown haired gal I bottled up too long. Here's to uncorking a bigger and better version of myself. I just hope it doesn't take me another twenty five years to accept the vintage.

But who knows, by then, I may end up with a few racing stripes, rear spoiler and if all goes well, a new engine.

Aunt Libby's Squash Casserole

If there's one thing we have plenty of in the summer here in Kentucky, it's yellow squash. Crookneck or straight neck it doesn't matter. Just fresh and not frozen is key. My Aunt Libby and my Mama made this as a regular dish around our homes. Cheap, delicious and when layered with cheese and sausage, you can use it for breakfast or dinner. I've even had it as a midnight snack. (like most foods in my house- The mushrooms were my own addition)

Ingredients:
5-6 medium yellow squash
1 lb bulk sausage (any flavor- I like Sage best)
1 cup sliced raw mushrooms
1 diced onion
3 cups shredded yellow cheese (Colby, Cheddar)
½ sleeve of Saltines (crushed)
½ stick of butter
1/3 tsp pepper
1/3 tsp salt

Preheat oven to 350*

1. Wash squash and slice in 1/3 inch slices.
Bring one large pot of water and sliced squash to a boil.
Cook 7 minutes. Drain. Set aside to cool.

2. In a large skillet cook sausage, mushrooms, salt, pepper and onion over medium heat until sausage is no longer pink. Drain.

3. Grease a large oblong, glass baking dish.

4. Take ½ of cooked, drained, squash and form one layer in bottom of dish.

5. With 1/2 of sausage mixture make a layer on top of sliced squash.

6. Top with 1 cup of shredded cheese.

7. Repeat layering steps.

8. Top cheese layer with crushed Saltines and drizzle with ½ stick of melted butter. Cook at 350* for 30 minutes or until bubbly and brown.

Fishing for Words

:~:~:~:~:~:~:~:~:~:

"If people concentrated on the really important things in life, there'd be a shortage of fishing poles." ~Doug Larson

My Mama says I went on my first camping and fishing trip when I was two. I can't remember it, but she says I ate the Shell-Crackers and Bream that my sisters and Daddy caught in Dawson Springs as fast as she could fry them. I suppose I have had a love for fishing my entire life.

When I was young, it was not unusual to see my mother and father and our dog Boogie pull up in front of my school in a Ford truck and camper hauling a fishing boat packed and ready to go. The cooler would be full of cold corn-meal-fried chicken, Moms homemade potato salad, cottage cheese, sliced cantaloupe, tomatoes, two giant Tupperware salt and peppers, white bread, bologna, Coke-a-Colas and Red Delicious apples. Except for the egg and smoked sausage breakfasts, we would eat all of the above or part of it for each meal we had while we were away. There would be no fast food, no pre packaged lunches only the good stuff from home and the occasional Snickers or Slim Jim from the dock bait shop.

I always loved the bait shops. For me, they were as close to a pet store as I would get. Sometimes, because I was the official "Minnow catcher" I would choose a particular minnow as a pet and hope that if he were still left at the end of the trip I could have the honors of "setting him free" when we were done. Since I was the only child on our outings, I had to find my fun wherever I could.

While most kids my age were gathering in small herds at roller skating rinks and their first boy/girl parties on the weekends I was working on tying the perfect hook. While many kids were finding ways to get away from their parents, I was spending the entire weekend with mine, sitting quietly on a lake, getting sunburned, eating apples and drinking Coke from glass bottles and watching our jet black family dog bake in the sun. Boogie loved the boat, she would lie down in the sun and her hair would get so hot it felt as if it may catch on fire. When she got too hot, she would find a cool spot under the shade of the steering wheel.

We would leave our campsite just after breakfast, and pack up our small cooler and head to the Marina while the fog was still coming off the lake. Fish would be jumping near the bank and ducks would just be entering the water after a nights sleep under the evergreens and bramble. With the suns rising, the heat would sear through my shirt onto my sunburned shoulders from my previous day on the lake. I can still feel the crinkle of my burnt nose when I squinted from the glorious dawn and the promise another day of fishing would bring.

My parents always said we were "Crappie Fishermen", and that is what we aimed for, but in reality, we would keep anything we could eat. We would feast on dinners of Bass, Bluegill, Crappie, Bream, Catfish, Shell-Crackers and Perch. The only ones that didn't make it to our table were the undersized and the un-delicious. We did not discriminate when it came to setting the table.

We would run into a few fishermen when we went on our trips that were trying to "get away" from the kids and wife, and Daddy would tell us that they were the ones missing out. He had the best anglers on the lake with him. I remember how good it made me feel that my Dad would rather be with his family than anyone else.

My mother was always the first one to catch a fish when we came to a new cove or found a new spot on the lake. She was our official fish detector. If after a few moments Mom didn't have her bait stolen, nearly lose her pole or reel in a "keeper" we moved on. At one point, I remember my mother catching two fish at once. She had a line with two hooks, at two depths and caught two Crappies at the same time.

My father was always fun to watch. He was the "he-man" of the boat, he would guide us back into the coves full of stick ups and trees. He tied us up to trees that were riddled with Woodpecker holes, draped with spider webs and dotted with wasp nests and point us in the right direction for a cast or to drop a line.

He took so much care getting us back in the thickets that by the time he would settle in he would be the first to lose his pole or get a line stuck. This would make him so frustrated and when he would reach to pull his line free, Mom and I learned to hide our heads and bend forward so that we wouldn't lose an eye. He had caught us in the front of our shirts before and even nearly lost an ear himself from a line that shot back from his fierce casts.

I miss those days on the lakes and rivers. I lost my first molar on a Marathon candy bar in the middle of Kentucky Lake. I learned to drive a boat before I learned to drive a car. I can tell the difference between a regular bass and a Kentucky bass and I spent more quality time with my parents than any kid I knew.

I am so thankful for those times on the water, those hours of quiet that taught me to appreciate the simple satisfaction of a well placed cast and the excitement of not knowing what was waiting on the other side.

Kentucky Hot Brown Casserole

First made popular at the Famous Brown Hotel, the Kentucky Hot Brown is nothing short of a culinary staple and an edible icon of the Bluegrass State. The mixture of flavors is celestial, even if they have been altered a bit for this recipe for a make-ahead family meal. The simple combinations of white sauce, parmesan, turkey and bacon topped with fresh tomatoes; well it does a body good. It may even make you appreciate Kentucky fare more than you ever realized was possible!

Ingredients:

5-6 slices of white bread. Toasted lightly and cubed.
1 cup of cooked Turkey. Cubed.
2 cups of cooked ham. Cubed. (If at all possible 1 cup of this should be precooked Country Ham)
1 pkg of cooked bacon. Crumbled.
2 fresh tomatoes sliced ¼" thin (homegrown and/or ripe)
1 cup of cheddar cheese (Sharp or Extra Sharp)
4 1/2 cups of milk (2% or whole)
5 Tbs butter
9 Tbs flour
1 1/3 cup of grated or shredded Parmesan Cheese

1. Preheat oven to 350*
2. Combine Turkey and Ham and set aside.
3. In saucepan, melt Butter on Medium. Add Flour. Cook and stir constantly with whisk until thick, sizzling and creamy.
4. Add milk slowly and cook mixture until thickened.
5. Add Cheddar cheese and whisk until cheese melts and sauce forms.
6. Place toasted cheese cubes in well-greased oblong baking dish.
7. Top bread with turkey/ham combination.
8. Pour cheese sauce over top of bread.
9. Sprinkle with crumbled bacon.
10. Add thin tomato slices.

11. Top with Parmesan cheese.
12. Bake at 350* for 25-30 minutes or until casserole is bubbly and browned. Serves 6.

Sweatin' with the "oldie"

:~:~:~:~:~:~:~:~:~:~:~:~:~:

"and you may ask yourself...how did I get here?"
~The Talking Heads (David Byrne)

I laid out my clothes as if I were going to an interview, making sure I had coordinating shirt and pants, clean socks for later, and a change of clothes. Carefully I rolled up my clean clothes and placed them in my gym bag. It had arrived, my first day back to the gym in over two years...

I couldn't even find my gym identification card, which was a good indicator of my priorities up until this point. That loss will cost me fifteen bucks to replace, this trip was already getting expensive, especially after buying new tennis shoes and tee shirts.

I don't even know how I got to this point. How did I go from being a size 12 in my wedding dress to nearly the largest size in the Women's-plus department? I know that it is entirely my fault of course, there is no force feeding done here at the Rigneys. But, I am not sure how I arrived at this point so tired and self-defeated. Many times I have lost weight and temporarily won the battle only to let go again and put it all back on plus ten.

I have had a love affair with food my entire life. I have a mother who could make anything taste delicious. My young palate was tempted with the flavor of buffalo and elk to frog legs and Moose. I spent a lot of time helping my mother prepare food. We snapped beans together and did lots of chores in the kitchen. Sometimes I would just sit at the dinner table and color while she prepared dinner and told me stories of her life as a little girl in the kitchen.

The smells that emanated from that small kitchen were enormous. When she would draw the string for the fan over the stove to let out heat, everyone in the neighborhood got a whiff of what the Millers were having for dinner, and mouths watered in all directions.

Time spent preparing food is a connection with my mother, and I attach good times, and love with food. Kids used to spend time at their mothers apron strings nearly all day, because sometimes it took most of the afternoon to prepare the evening meal. I was not overweight when my mother cooked for me, she used whole foods and additives were non existent, food was good.

I have heard people say that dieting isn't as hard as trying to quit smoking, and if that is true, I'm glad I never smoked, or I would be one *ginormous* smoldering chunk, I would probably smoke in my sleep.

I am awful at dieting.

When I diet, all I think about is my next meal, and the one after that. All I imagine is how I can squeeze the largest amount of food into the smallest calories or carbohydrates. Once I even contemplated eating 2 jars of mushrooms, just to see how I could fill myself on nearly 0 carbs and calories. I think I am what they call a "volume eater", someone that needs to feel full. I thought about stomach-band surgery. But then I worried that I would have a panic attack worrying about plastic parts inside my body, I can barely tolerate tight underwear.

But, I have realized, the busier I am, the less I eat, the more I exercise I get the better I sleep and the less stressed I am. So that is why this previously sedentary gal has decided to be healthier and move more, and maybe just maybe I can forget about my food addiction and rise above it. This is what prompted my workout.

When I arrived at the gym, I felt as out of place as a Sumo wrestler at ballet class. I am sure no one cared or even noticed the sweat forming on my brow, but when the tops of my hands began to sweat, I was well aware of how out of shape I had become. I didn't even know there were sweat glands there. At one point, I just prayed that I didn't pass out and I wish I had slipped an aspirin in my lycra pocket in case my heart gave out before I finished. I remembered that my husband mentioned that when he has been to the gym and seen anyone who was struggling with their weight, how much he admired them for their effort and their courage to try. He also said I am perfect the way I am. God bless that man, even if he is lying, those words are what managed to get me through my mini workout and keep me from running to my car.

After my time was up, and I had finished my round on the elliptical, a great feeling came over me. Not only was I thrilled that it was over, but I felt a great sense of accomplishment and pride for having done my best. Sure, I could have quit when I felt out of place, or when I felt tired, but I pushed through and that made me feel good about me.

Now that summer is on its way, I get my workouts outdoors. I golf whenever I can, chase my daughter constantly, garden daily and mow the lawn once a week. I feel like I am moving more and eating less. I'll try to keep busy and maybe when I return to the gym in the Fall I will take up less space...which reminds me, I'll need a new gym card.

3 Green Casserole

This is a good sized healthy (somewhat) and tasty vegetable dish that makes a great potluck addition to a boring buffet. People feel good about eating vegetables, even if there is a little Mayo in this dish, it still won't be too filling.

Ingredients:

2 pkgs. of frozen French style green beans*

1 pkg. frozen peas*

1 pkg. frozen lima beans*

*(Cook vegetables according to package directions in one pan and drain well after cooking.)

To the cooked/drained vegetables add the following:

1 ½ tsp of Worcestershire sauce

1 ½ tsp lemon juice

1 cup of Mayonnaise

1 ½ tsp Mustard

1 white onion (chopped fine)

1 can of drained, sliced, water chestnuts

Directions:

1. Pour the vegetable mix into a well greased oblong glass dish (9 x13)

2. Top with crushed saltines or seasoned bread crumbs.

3. Bake at 350* for 40 minutes.

Thankful, thankful Thankfulness
:~:~:~:~:~:~:~:~:~:~:~:~:~:

"That I may publish with the voice of Thanksgiving, and tell of all thy wondrous works"...
                                            ~Psalms 26:7

I have so much to be thankful for. Sometimes I forget. One Thanksgiving weekend a few years ago it took a series of unfortunate and difficult events to remind me. Two rounds of Strep throat for our wee one, seven mercury filling replacements, a broken molar, two sinus infections, a car burglary and a sick family dog definitely made me wake up and take notice of my former catatonic appreciation of all things sweet and simple...

It all began with my decision to have my seven mercury fillings in my teeth replaced. After having them since age thirteen, I decided to part company with them in one fell swoop to our local dentist. He informed me that it was a lot of work to do in one day, but I knew if I didn't do them all at once, I probably would never get the rest done. After all, I am the woman with only one ear double-pierced. (It just hurt too much)

So, there I was with my "in for a dime, in for a dollar" philosophy in place and psyched up for my *Haz-mat* mercury removal. Not realizing the next 12 hours I would spend looking as though I had just suffered a small stroke. I had enough epinephrine in my body from the five numbing injections to fight off an army of bee stings and my tongue was bitten more times than I can count along with my tenderized cheek. I couldn't even speak for hours. But I was convinced it was all worth it.

What followed during the next two weeks was nothing short of chaos. That Friday, my daughter Lydia was diagnosed with Strep throat and on the way to fill her prescription, every parents automobile nightmare came true...nausea in the car.

For some reason, children are not drawn to open car windows when they are nauseous, instead they prefer the inside route. Even when being nearly pushed out the window by a parent trying to maneuver their Earth Destroyer 9000 to the nearest parking lot, they will undoubtedly gain super-strength and recoil back into the upholstered interior and hover over electronic door controls, speakers and hand rests to relieve themselves.

That being said, I raced home with windows cracked and swore neither of us would ever eat eggs for breakfast again. Once inside the house, she gave a repeat performance in my bed which was followed by a Phenergan-suppository-induced coma.

After cleaning the car, bed and carpets, thanks to better living through chemistry *Typhoid Mary* was improving and I prepared myself for the weekend I had been looking forward to. I sat down with my family to watch a movie and just as I bit into my first handful of Orville's best buttery popcorn, I cracked a newly restored molar. Of course since it was the weekend, the dentist was closed, nothing ever happens during business hours. So, I spent the next 48 hours with my tongue over my serrated tooth to protect it from all things hot, cold or in-between and severed nearly every taste bud from the right side of my tongue in the process.

Right after this event, before the movie was even over, my oldest son had a bracket break on his new braces.

Yay, I'll have company for my interstate car trip to my least favorite place.

But all hope was not lost, a new cap for my tooth was in my future and I left with a temporary from my dental office the following Monday. Not so bad really. I felt like I needed to look at the positive, Lydia was back in school and I wasn't looking like a wild mountain woman from the holler now that I was no longer sporting a toothless grin.

A few days passed and things were perking up, then along came Fall in Kentucky and one of the worst sinus infections I have ever had, in fact, I think I still have it. That Friday, Lydia woke up "extra crispy" from a returning fever and after a tear-filled throat culture we found that her Strep had indeed returned, with a vengeance. After enduring yet another weekend of fevers and shared illness I woke on Monday morning and found my Earth Destroyer 9000 had been burglarized in our driveway. After giving a police report I was given a warning that my car tags had expired by the attending officer and this was followed by taking one Wee Rigney late to school and incurring another tardy for her attendance record. I had started yet another week with a mark against me.

Thinking that it had to get better, I rested my weary, congested, post nasal drip head only to wake to a very sick "*Sweet Tea*", our forty pound wiener dog. Not only had she eaten a cheeseburger wrapper that had blown into the garage from someone's overturned garbage can up the street, she had also ingested a chicken thigh bone the night before, stolen from the plate of a certain teenager that shall remain nameless.

Don't let anyone tell you that God doesn't have a sense of humor.

So, I sat bent and a bit twisted at the end of a three week survival camp filled with strep throats, congested sinuses, broken braces, a cracked molar, a defiled and burgled SUV and a sickly red-haired-wiener-wolf. After a brief bout of crying, I forced myself to be thankful.

Way too often, I have found myself saying, "*Why me?*" Probably more times than I can count I have held pity parties for myself and called upon the wise words of my mother. Her most often used phrase is "*This too shall pass*" and up until now I didn't allow those words to offer me much comfort. Now I find a great amount of strength in them.

Just saying them to myself, I felt much better. I had a tough three weeks but my children fully recovered, I still have my my health; albeit poor at the moment and my dog has survived her gourmet meal of wax paper and chicken bone.

Life is good.

So, perhaps next Thanksgiving as we all bend our head in prayer I should thank God for teaching me that a happy life doesn't lie in anything more than the love and health of your loved ones and the well-being of the family dog.

However, if I do forget again, I hope I can learn my lesson without Pine scented disinfectant and Children's Tylenol.

Best Ever Cranberry Relish with Red, Red Wine

I love cooking with wine. Especially the reds. I just recently started enjoying good hearty reds with meals and if you have a particularly robust red this is the perfect recipe to use that little cup or two you have left. Wine brings out the character of the cranberry in a way that I never realized. I had only had cranberry relish with sugar before but by adding the red wine, the deep snap of the cranberry is in every bite and the orange zest really keeps the tongue on its toes. This is so tasty that it is a great topping for Vanilla Bean ice cream too.

Ingredients:
1 1/3 cups sugar
½ cup of water
1 cup red wine (a red zinfandel or a merlot will do fine)
1 package of fresh cranberries. Rinsed and drained.
1-2 Cinnamon sticks
2 and ½ Tbs Orange zest.

1. In a medium saucepan, bring sugar, water and wine to a boil over medium heat.
2. Add cranberries, cinnamon and orange zest.
3. Return to boil, the reduce heat to a simmer.
4. Cook, stirring often until all the cranberries have burst. This takes about 10 minutes.
5. Remove pan from heat and let relish to cool to room temperature. Then pour into container and refrigerate overnight. Serve hot or cold the next day.

Stand and deliver
:~:~:~:~:~:~:~:~:~:~:~:

"Life's what you make it" ~anonymous

Once, I was asked to write a memorial about a friend of mine who had died unexpectedly. After my writing was complete and I read what I had written, I stood in awe of the legacy of love and laughter this person had left to their family and friends. Even though a life had been interrupted in its prime, it had made the world a better place.

Later, I had to ask myself what my legacy was, and what could be said about me and what I stand for when I am gone? Over the months prior, I had a reawakening of sorts, due to some health issues that managed to shake me up a bit and force me to see how fragile life is, how precious each day is, and the importance of being true to your self.

How would you live your life if you knew each day could be your last? Would you change anything? Would you live it differently? I asked myself these questions and found that although the questions are simple in nature, the answers were much more complex.

I love my life, the good, the bad and the difficult. So, at first I wasn't sure if I would change anything other than taking more time with my children, more time away from the television and finding more opportunities just to hold David's hand on a quiet walk.

For the most part I belong to a happy go lucky and extremely loud clan. I can't remember a day I haven't told my children that I love them or a day where I haven't let my husband know how much he means to me. Laughter abounds in the Rigney household.

From a very early age, I have learned to celebrate life's little pleasures. I once had someone tell me that I could *"make friends with a rock"* and I consider that a compliment. But if I look deeper, I find that I have a pretty long list of faults. I get frustrated with the kids too fast, and I could probably use a good dose of patience most of the time. I fuss and fume and only recently began paying attention to my health.

I am learning to appreciate my body regardless of its size, and honestly, it's difficult. I used to base a lot of how I felt about my world on my appearance and seeing myself as only an overweight woman and not much else, made it hard to embrace the glory of being alive. I chose surrendering my self-esteem and giving in to self-doubt over appreciating the fact that I was blessed with the love of a wonderful family and a beautiful life. That was a very selfish thing to do, because having a poor image of myself, could affect how my children feel about themselves, and they are wonderful and perfect just like they are. So that is something I decided a while ago to work on, and I am so thankful that I can make that journey. Although I am overweight, there is more to me than that. I am surely more than how much space I take up in the world, and my dress size.

I began this final chapter asking myself what type of legacy I would like to leave, and now I realize that it's more important to be a "living" legacy. Not only worrying about how I am going to be remembered 50 years from now, but more importantly how I'm going to be remembered after I leave a room, hang up a phone or close a door. I want to stand for something everyday, leave people with a smile on their face and see promise in my world. For so many of us, myself included, we worry too much about the superficial things in life, how small our bodies are and how many material things we are piling up in our own little corner of this vast universe. We all want what everyone else has, wonder what our own inheritances will be, what we will leave behind that is worth something by sizing it up to the mighty dollar. All this matters very little when you think about it.

After looking at it this way, I feel blessed just to wake up each morning in a warm bed surrounded by people who love me, in spite of me.

After getting my "all clear" from my doctor after battling Thyroid Cancer a few years ago, my family had a Cancer-Free party for me. My oldest son William came to me afterwards and said, *"Why all the fuss mama? You're so much more than this. Surely kicking cancer's butt isn't your greatest accomplishment...you've raised three kids and you've got a great marriage. You life is much more than Margie-Cancer survivor."* He was right. It really put things into perspective for me. My struggles, my challenges involve everyone that loves me, everyone that I love. My life is tangled into the lives of others.

So will I change my life? Will I live it differently? I want to continue to build a better me, from the inside out. I want to make each day count, but be able to forgive myself and others when those days seem long and difficult. Whenever possible, I want to build my children up with my words and not tear them down. I want them to see that life is great and precious and that by finding joy in their own strengths and weaknesses they will be celebrating their own lives to their fullest.

It's okay to be wrong, it's okay to say you're sorry and it's okay to forgive, you do that for yourself. You may not be able to keep the relationships you have that hurt you or stressed you, but you can move on and move past the anger and the resentments.

I heard an old saying once, *"inside every person, there's a good book"*, and I want my life to represent that idea. Life is too short to worry about what we're going to leave behind.

So for me, I'll choose to embrace the good, the bad and the ugly of it and who knows, maybe I'll live an unpublished *best seller.*

Granny Miller's Mayonnaise Drop Biscuits

I saved my most beloved recipe for last. These biscuits are the first thing I ever made on my own. My Granny wrote down this simple recipe on a small corner of an envelope for me once when I helped her stir the biscuits on Sunday afternoon.

Whenever I eat them I'm eight years old again, sitting in my Granny's kitchen on her favorite step-stool. Watching her cook, wiping her hands on her apron front and waiting for my Papaw to come in and steal a slice of roast before dinner is ready. In this temporary day dream, I'm surrounded by the smells of pork gravy, cooked potatoes and green beans 'n ham. I can see the sweat forming beads from the steam of cooked potatoes and beans on the sliding glass door that leads to the back porch. In my daydream, her house is full of family. My family. Some are waiting in the living room, some are on the porch and some are in the den. All in anxious anticipation as these biscuits will be the last thing needed before the dinner bell rings.

I loved my Granny. If it's possible, I think I love her more now than ever even though she has been gone for nearly twenty years. Sometimes I feel like she is by my side in the kitchen when I use something that belonged to her or create a dish from one of her recipes. Often the smell of her Rose Milk hand lotion will pass through my house and it makes me think of her. The first thing I ever made from my Granny's recipes were these moist Mayonnaise Drop Biscuits. She was the first person that introduced me to baking mixes and I use them all the time as a short cut for pancakes, biscuits and pot pie crusts.

Aside from my mother, she is the greatest cook I have ever known.

Ingredients:
2 and 1/2 cups of Baking Mix (Jiffy, Bisquick or store brand)
2/3 cup of milk
1/2 cup of Real Mayonnaise
   1. Heat oven to 450*. Stir in baking mix, milk and mayonnaise

until soft dough forms. (If too wet, add a touch of baking mix)
2. Drop dough by soft, sticky, spoonfuls onto greased or non stick cookie sheet.
3. Bake 8-10 minutes or until golden brown.

Biography

Hello. My name is Margie Rigney. I grew up in the heart of the Bluegrass. I'm happily married to my wonderful husband David and mother to three beautiful people; William, Ben and Lydia.

Food is my friend. Rumor has it I've never met a casserole I didn't like. Good food has been my companion throughout my life and at times, it's been my salvation.

The idea of combining my love for writing about life with recipes came to me one day after I realized I had a tendency to romanticize about food in much of my work. Oftentimes, something I wrote would actually make me hungry. So the idea for a peek-into-the-life-of-moi, "foodie" book was born.

I was always taught the pathway to anyone's heart begins at the kitchen door. Recipes passed down from generation to generation should be considered treasured artifacts. These relics are an edible history of our family trees. Most of the recipes in this book have been handed down, made up out of necessity or I've reworked recipes to satisfy my family's own tastes and preferences. Never be afraid to try new things, if you're not an onion lover, leave them out. Take a recipe and make it your own, simply by changing a few ingredients you can create a culinary masterpiece.

I got my first apron before I was four years old and I haven't stopped wearing one since. While most women may not aspire to be June Cleaver, you gotta admire a gal that can do it all in heels and pearls and still have time for the beauty parlor.

I have a tendency to laugh at myself more than most people. I quit worrying about what people thought of me for my fortieth birthday present. I've learned the hard way that life is precious and it's too short to spend worrying about people and things you can't control.

For me, it's always the perfect time to pop a cork, crack a good cookbook and stir things up.

Margie M. Rigney

Other works by Margie M. Rigney coming soon:

"The Fat Suit-*confessions of an overweight housewife*"

&

"Mama Never Told Me There'd be Days like This"

www.ingramcontent.com/pod-product-compliance
Lightning Source LLC
Chambersburg PA
CBHW051832090426
42736CB00011B/1765